# Memoirs of a Grandad (a happy life in 5 fits)

**To my Mom Shirley, thank you for bringing me into this world and my dear wife Mel who has put up with me all of these years...**

Published By Lord Kenburn Books, England.

Copyright © 2021 David Hughes (Lord Kenburn)

All rights reserved. No part of this publication may be reproduced, distributed, or transmitted in any form or by any means, including photocopying, recording, or other electronic or mechanical methods, without the prior written permission of the publisher, except in the case of brief quotations embodied in critical reviews and certain other noncommercial uses permitted by copyright law. For permission requests, contact David Hughes at lordkenburn@protonmail.com

Ordering Information: For details, contact lordkenburn@protonmail.com or Amazon.com

Print ISBN: 9798745818462

Printed in the United Kingdom. First Edition.

## **CONTENTS**

**Preface- Back in The Days of Tanners and Bobs**

**Fit One - The Earliest of Days.**

**Fit Two- Secondary School.**

**Fit Three- Becoming a Young Man.**

**Fit Four- Learning Chinese.**

**Fit 5- Everything Will be Alright in The End.**

**Epilogue - This Grandad's brief history.**

## **Preface**

Back in the days of Tanners and Bobs,
When Mothers had patience and Fathers had jobs.
When football team families wore hand me down shoes,
And T.V. gave only two channels to choose.
Back in the days of threepenny bits,
when schools employed nurses to search for your nits.
When snowballs were harmless: ice slides were permitted
And all of your jumpers were warm and hand knitted.
Back in the days of hot ginger beers,
When children remained so for more than six years.
When children respected what older folks said,
And pot was a thing you kept under your bed.
Back in the days of 'Watch with Mother',
When neighbours were friendly and talked to each other.
When cars were so rare you could play in the street.
When Doctors made house calls and police walked the beat.
Back in the days of 'Milligan's Goons',
When butter was butter and songs all had tunes.
It was dumplings for dinner and trifle for tea,
and your annual break was a day by the sea.
Back in the days of Dixon's Dock Green,
Crackerjack pens and Lyon's ice cream.

When children could freely wear National Health glasses,
and teachers all stood at the FRONT of their classes
Back in the days of rocking and reeling,
When mobiles were things that you hung from the ceiling.
When woodwork and pottery got taught in schools,
and everyone dreamed of a win on the pools.
Back in the days when I was a lad,
I can't help but smile for the fun that I had.
Hopscotch and roller skates; snowballs to lob.
Back in the days of Tanners and Bobs.

Anon.

## **Foreword**

This work isn't a song or poem but I decided to use the term 'fit' as that is how my recollections feel looking back over my life thus far. These memoirs have been 61 years in the making and were finally compiled and written during my isolation during the Covid 19 pandemic of 2020/2021. I would like the reader to bear in mind that some of the terms and references used are from a past era and today could be misunderstood or cause offence. I will apologise in advance if any of the references cause offence as that is not meant in any way. Finally, I have been careful, as far as possible, not to mention any actual place names or people's names, however they will instantly recognise both if they ever get to read this work.

## Fit One: The Earliest of Days

Well apparently, according to Google, I was born on a Thursday 533,482 hours ago from today. Although by the time you read this, the clock of life will have moved on a while and those hours, minutes and seconds will have increased. I was born in a hospital in Nottingham, a place I cannot remember anything about except 'The Legend of Robin Hood', whom I had nothing in common with.

My earliest recollections would have been from about 2 years old where I lived in a small South Staffordshire village in my GrandParent's rented place. They lived in a tiny cottage with one room downstairs and two bedrooms upstairs.

Bed room one was occupied by my parents and me and the small bedroom to the left up the stairs was where my maternal Nan and Grandad slept. You gained access to the upstairs by a flight of stairs which led directly from the only downstairs room. This was a big living room containing: a well worn two seater settee, two arm chairs, a coin operated black & white TV and a large hearth containing an (ever lit) open fire, even during the summer months. This was the cottage's only source of heating.

To the left of the room, was an archway that led into a tiny kitchen which contained a two ring electric hob with an oven underneath. This area always smelt musty and the room always seemed to have the whitewash covering peeling from the ceiling. To the right of the room, a door led down a large stone step into a brewhouse where we used to fill a metal pail from a very large brass tap. This was then brought into the room and used as drinking water. The brewhouse contained an old stone Belfast type sink, which is where we washed ourselves, cleaned and washed the clothes and dirty kitchen utensils.

If you continued down the stone step, turned right and exited the brewhouse beside the very large brass tap secured on a stone sink, you came to a bricked yard which contained two red bricked buildings. Both of these you had to pass to continue down a path and 100 yards to go to a third building (which my Grandad referred to as 'going up the back' . This was in fact our toilet. If you got taken short, you had no chance and filled your pants by the time you reached the first of these buildings. I will come to what lived in the second building later but the first building's occupant was a very large and angry looking dog called Jip. He was chained to the building with a heavy chain and would rush forward as you passed him, barking and snarling inspiring you to break into a sprint to outrun the reach of his chain, which was useful to get you to the toilet faster if the need arose. This happened quite often having encountered Jip.

The toilet was a little red brick building with a black slate tiled roof. It had two doors to the front which creaked wearily when opened. Both doors were rickety and painted with brown paint that was flakey and peeling. The first door (the one on the left) was ours and the other? Well, apparently owned by the people down the street. I never saw these people however they were a complete mystery.

When you entered, directly in front of you was a bench-like seat with a wooden top and two wooden holes. Each hole continued down to a large metal can full of excrement. It then became apparent that the toilet was in fact two joined toilets. I often wondered what would happen if I was in mid flow and the person down the road decided to use their toilet too. Also why were there two doors when they led to the same place? The place absolutely stank of a stale, sweet and sticky decomposing mess. In the summer months, you could in fact smell this from inside the cottage. It was even worse on a Monday, as a man from the Rural District Council used to arrive in a maroon coloured van and carry a weeks worth of whatever in two cans from the toilets (one over each shoulder) and empty them into the back of the vehicle. I never looked at what he emptied them into but the contents of the cans made a sloshing noise as he carried them and spilled over his broad shoulders, dripping down his back. I remember thinking that when I grow up I don't want to do that for a living.

Thinking about that then, there was another career I realised I did not want to pursue. This brings me back to what was in the second low brick building. It contained a pig. A noisy and most smelly creature which was fed with all the scraps of food we didn't eat. My Grandmother used to buy them as a little piglet but they soon grew into an enormous creature and after 8 months frightened me so much. It was then a man in white overalls and a leather apron used to call with a large black bag. On that day, I was told to stay inside the house. This was good for many reasons but in particular to avoid the noise. A loud sickly scream, that to me felt like fingernails scraping down a blackboard, would go on for about a minute, then you could hear loud bangs and then nothing. Silence and peace with birdsong in the air.

That first time must have been in May 1963 as I remember hearing one of the first songs I can ever remember, 'I like it' by Gerry and the Pacemakers. The sound of which wafted across to my ears from Bob the butcher's transistor radio, which he used to place upon the pigsty wall. The musical sounds would accompany him, in a macabre sort of way, whilst he did his grizzly deeds. Whenever I hear that song today I am transported back to that moment in time.

Magically, the next day the beast was gone and in its place a lovely little piglet. "Amazing", I used to think. Years later, I realised that the man in white was in fact Bob the butcher from the local butcher's shop and the provider of mobile abattoir services. I won't go into too much detail, however for the next 3 months we seemed to eat a lot of bacon, black pudding, sausages, pork joints and strange offaly things which I didn't know the names of at the time.

Past the toilet block I mentioned a few moments ago, and to the left led another path. This led to my Grandad's vegetable plot and beyond that a pigeon pen in which he kept his 'prize 'racing pigeons. Yes he was, in his spare time a pigeon fancier.

He would proudly stuff two of his birds into a wicker basket on a Friday evening and walk to the local village pub. There a congregation of other village men would meet and consume large amounts of Banks's beer. Then at about 9pm a large lorry (called a pigeon transporter) would arrive and a silence descended upon the group. The seriousness of the business would start.

Firstly, each pigeon would have the pub's address stamped upon their wing (using a John Bull printing set) Then a ring with a number etched upon it, would be put on it's leg. If I had been a good lad all week, I was the one to place the rings upon their fragile legs carefully securing the ring in place with a pair of pliers. The ring had a number which I read out to the Secretary of the group (otherwise known as my Dad). He would then enter this into a large leather bound book next to the name of the pigeon, whether it was a cock or a hen and the owner's name.

The pigeon was then placed into a larger wicker basket with 15 other pigeons and then that was loaded onto the lorry. The secretary then pressed a button upon a carriage type looking clock (called a stop clock). Each pigeon owner had one of these. This was an important piece of equipment as, when, or more likely if, your pigeon returned from the impending lorry ride you needed to catch the pigeon and take off its ring and then place the ring into the clock in order to stop it. The time taken could then be registered the following Friday when you presented your clock for inspection and a winner declared. The meeting would end at about 10pm with the lorry driving off to some far flung corner of the UK or Europe.

By the following Wednesday, some of the pigeons would start returning home. That is where the fun started as the owner, in this case, my Grandad had to lure the pigeon down from the roof in order to retrieve the ring and then stop the clock. Time was valuable as in many cases the prize money for winning was high and also a regular winning bird became very valuable when put out to stud. Unfortunately for them, most of my Grandad's birds ended up in the stewpot. He would try everything to lure his prize possessions down from the roof. Strange cooing and clucking noises he would make which became louder and descended into verbal abuse and threats if the bird was still up there after 40 minutes. Not to mention some of the exquisite hand gestures he used to make. He would use expensive feeds and potions to lure the feathered beast down but always the pigeon knew best and would fly down when he wanted to.

Often many of his pigeons would turn up many days late and my Grandad used to hold them in his hand and with a wry smile say "you won't see him again" however, you did see him again, a few days later in a stew. Strange 58 years later what sticks in your mind.

I seemed to spend a lot of time with older members of my family. Mainly because Mom and Dad were busy and the older relatives would 'babysit' the oldest child (that was me for a time). I found older people fascinating as most of them were born in the late 1800s when Queen Victoria was on the throne. They had lived through so much. The stories they told me were always truly fascinating about how things had changed and how things were so much better back then.

It is a strange thing, the passage of time, as I sit here today I realise that I am a similar age to them now. I now have 2 children of my own and 3 grandchildren and wonder if they enjoy my stories, many of which they have probably heard a hundred times or more. My world is so different to that of my grandchildren as was mine growing up back then, compared to that of my Grandparents, Great Aunts and Great Uncles.

Stories that stick out in my mind from the time include my Great Uncle (my Grandad's elder brother) telling me of his first love long ago. He used to ride a horse to visit her some 5 miles away every Sunday. To impress her, once a month, he would borrow the local farmer's horse and buggy and take her a ride in the surrounding countryside. On the one occasion he asked me to guess what she did for a living. I think I had tried all professions, all of which he had answered with that wry smile of his shaking his head and inviting me to have another guess. He said he wouldn't tell me and that I had to guess.

I asked him one day why he had married my Great Aunt and not this lady he so often talked about. It was clear in my mind looking back that he had deep affections for her. However he always talked about her in the past tense. Then, surprisingly, one day he explained she had passed away suddenly whilst she was at work. He explained he was devastated as he didn't find out for over a week after it had happened.

"What happened?" I asked, awaiting a sad explanation involving a road accident or something falling on her head at work. But what he told me next made me laugh. I know you shouldn't laugh at or about death but her cause of death was utterly unbelievable, especially in a South Staffordshire village.

"Well" he sighed putting his head in his hands "she was eaten by a lion!" For you see she was a lion tamer. He didn't tell me the later of course but I put two and two together. He then asked me never to tell anyone. I did however, many years later tell this story to my wife and later to my children and grandchildren, but I am sure they don't believe it. It must have been a true story as old people don't tell lies do they?

One of the most vivid memories I have is of my Nan (my Mom's mother) was of her buying me a notebook and pencil. She told me it was to pass the time when I was bored. When I did get bored she would tell me to sit on the large sandstone step outside the front door of her cottage. When a vehicle drove past to use my pencil to write down the number of the registration plate.

Now, as you may have guessed, there weren't many vehicles in the countryside back then but I suppose on a good day I would note down about 20. After a few days of doing this, you got to see the same vehicles going past at about the same time. My Dad, when he saw what I was doing, advised me to add another dimension to my note taking activities.

He had recently joined the AA and received an AA handbook. Within its many pages, was a section on car registrations plates and how you could tell the year the car was first registered and where the vehicle came from. Fascinating I thought and I redesigned my noted book with two extra columns. This new found hobby was to become a part of my life for the next 7 years or so and was particularly exciting when my Mom and Dad started to venture further afield during my parents holidays and days off. I got to recognise all the plates from all over the UK without having to look them up. Yes I know so sad some may think, but heck I really had some fun back then, without spending a penny.

The next part of my life I remember vividly is my primary school days at St John's Church of England Primary School, especially my first day and my attempt at escaping in the back of the dinner van.

It must have been early September 1965 and I remember being walked up the lane, by my Mom and past a row of terraced cottages to the village school right next to the church. In fact that lane was called Church Lane. I will mention the church again a little later. For now, we arrived for my first day at the village school, complete with a world war two relic: an air raid shelter!!

This was the very same school that mom, my grandad and great grandad had attended many years before. There were only 3 teachers and the vicar as it was such a small, Church of England, village school. Each teacher would teach the same class for class for 2 years and then you would move to the next class and so on until you would have to attend the 'big' school in the next village. My Maths wasn't that great but I worked out that would mean spending the next 6 years of my life in the somber looking 'penitentiary.'

A few weeks earlier, I remember being fitted for my uniform with a bottle green cap and a brown leather satchel to boot. It all felt itchy and scratchy but I guessed I must have looked cute from the looks my Mom gave me! "Oh no!" I thought when I saw other children, "'Do I have to make friends with them?", as to date the only people I had mixed with were my parents, grandparents, great aunts, great uncles, Jip, pigeons and pigs. The latter would come and go though as did Jip eventually.

Now just to digress a little here, some of the men in my family had served in the military in World War 2 and, as it had finished only less than 20 years before, stories were still rife. The film everyone was talking about at the time was the 1963 film 'The Great Escape'. I was too young, it was felt, to go to the cinema and see this at the time but a lot of the men folk in the family had and I had listened to their versions of what they had viewed. It was screened on the black and white TV two years later in 1965.

Anyway, back to the first day at school and I had heard that at 12 noon a hot lunch would be delivered in a van. I didn't want that sort of lunch as my mom had put sandwiches into my new satchel. She called that a packed lunch. So when the bell rang at 10 to 12 (a proper old, brass school bell rung by the headmistress) I went outside and saw this van approach through the school gate and grind to a halt. A man (later to be known as the school diner man) wearing a long, dark coat got out and opened the back of the van. He then made 3 trips from the van and into the school carrying boxes, presumably containing food for the children who were taking school lunch. I watched the school diner man carry in his 3rd load of rations and then put my cunning plan into operation.

Checking that no enemy was in sight, I snuck in via the open back double doors of the van and moved forward, camouflaging myself under a large blanket hoping that 'the Germans' wouldn't see. Sure enough, the Nazi prison warder (aka the school dinnerman) returned and pushed some empty boxes in the back which aided my disguise. The door was shut firmly. I heard a murmering from out side, the driver's door being opened and the Nazi climbed aboard and started the engine, reversing a short distance and then turning the vehicle so that he faced forward meaning he could drive out of the school gates whose rusted squeaky hinges I could hear from my hide. I felt the van go forward and a slight bump as the vehicle moved over the lowered kerbstone and into the lane.

"Yes, I had done it" I thought and as soon as I am a safe distance away from this gulag I can make my escape whilst the Nazi is distracted at a stop sign and negotiate my cunning stunt over the hills to a neutral Switzerland (otherwise known as the village green. Well that was the thinking behind it but not quite what happened next. Well, he must have heard me move or seen me in his rear view mirror so he slammed on the brakes and the van ground to a halt. Without saying anything, he turned the vehicle around in the middle of the road and headed immediately back to the school.

"Has he missed one of his boxes?" I wondered, but in fact no, he had seen me! He returned me safely back through the school gates and handed me over to a red faced, very angry headmistress. I was frog marched into her office and received a very stern telling off. I then spent the whole of that first afternoon writing 'I must not do it again' for what seemed like a 500 times...(because it was) on an A4 piece of paper (in fact 13 sides of A4 paper). I went home with a very sore arm which was followed by a very sore bottom courtesy of Mom and a very early night in bed with no tea. Safe to say I didn't try that again.

I was left alone and in the dark that night thinking, "Did you have a nice day at school David? Oh yes most eventful but I am glad it's all over now and think I won't bother going back there again and retire, just like my Grandad." You see, I want to be a lollipop man as you don't need to start work until you are 65. How wrong was I as later you will see my first job was at 13 and I am still working now at the age of 61. Yes I did go back to school the very next day and soon forgot about my lollipop wielding, chosen profession.

Life was fun and happy back then in that simple lifestyle and that lovely village where everyone knew each other. A village with its own policeman who would walk around at night and check everyone had locked up. The little Post Office, complete with a postmistress immaculately dressed who knew everyone and their business too. The little shop on the canal bridge that seemed to sell everything. Summers seemed hotter and winters colder as the time passed by in an instant.

The village had its own woodland, which seemed vast, and as children we played during the holidays and weekends from dawn until dusk. There was a cave in the woods which as kids we thought was haunted. Only the brave would go inside the dank darkness armed with a fern that we had pulled out of the ground and pretended would have defended us against any wild bears. No wild bears though, only silence and emptiness.

One Christmas, my Grandad bought me a torch and the first place I went was there. It was to be the first time I was able to go all of the way inside and see what was lurking in the shadows. No animals or ghosts but, to my amazement, I found my mom's name carved there into the sandstone like some prehistoric carving etched in time. There were many other names there too, past generations of village children that had visited over the years. I added my name there as well and I guess it is still there today, etched beneath that of my

Mom complete with the date: 26 December 1970. Another decade had passed.

I never did find out what the cave was for. Some said it was an old dwelling carved out by a hermit, others said the church silver was hidden in there during the war and another rumour was that it was an ice house. Its real use was never proven however and to this day I still do not know. Children today in that village probably never go there now as they are too busy on Sony Play Stations and computer games devoid of the pleasures of a more simpler life; or is that just my thinking?

## Fit Two:  Secondary School and Beyond.

There are times in your life when something significant happens and you can remember exactly where you were and what you were doing. For me two of the most vivid were: firstly, The Apollo Moon landing on 20 July 1969, where I sat up all night, viewing on a rented a black and white TV of Man's first steps on the Moon. That was remarkable. However it was  literally a world away and although noteworthy it was the events some 18 months later that got the whole county talking, decimalisation. That was my second vivid memory.

On 15 February 1971,  just 2 months later than my woodland escapade at the cave. What was going on?  Coins and notes we had been brought up with, were  disappearing and being replaced by new pence. The base 10, was a new way of thinking and doing things everyday. What, so now there would be 100 new pence to the pound and not 240 or 20 shillings as we had all grown up with?  Was this a devious plot to make money out of us?  Well my Grandad said it was and he must be right as he was a wise man in my eye. No more 10 bob notes from him for my birthdays. Goodness me you could do a lot with that back then but 50 pence today? well it doesn't go far does it?

The year 1971 was a poignant year for me also, in the fact that I started the BIG school. No more walking the five minutes to the little village school. Now, my early mornings would be a major adventure as instead of waking up at 8.30 am, I needed to be up and dressed by 7.30am. I then had to walk for 15 minutes in the opposite direction to the 'old school' and wait in the cold for the school bus to turn up at 8.10am. Well that was the plan but that old Charabanc, actually a 1950s old, and I mean old and shabby coach would arrive anytime between 8 am and 9am. It then travelled for 35 minutes through open countryside stopping to pick up other children from the next 2 villages enroute. A total compliment then of 50 or so children of varying ages in a 45 seater wreck with no seat belts. How things change!

The reason I knew that vehicle was from the 1950s was that my Mom did exactly as I was to do for the next 5 years, during her 5 years of schooling at the same secondary school and on the same mode of transport. She even said it was the same vehicle! She also said it was the same driver and also some of the teachers when I got to school would be the same teachers who taught her. 'Goodness me!' I thought, 'Is it a school or an old folks home?'

Compared to the little village school this was a huge, ivory towered palace and another day in my life I can remember vividly. One you were one of the biggest leaving the village to become one of the smallest in the new school, which had a sixth form and meant some of the students were 6 years older. My goodness 'old' people. So that was to be my life then for at least the next 5 years, maybe 6.

What I didn't know then, at the age of 11 in September 1971, is that by the end of that decade I would be married and my wife (who I would meet later at that same school) and I would buy our first property together. We are still together, over 40 years later, with two lovely daughters and 3 grandchildren, and we have had many adventures together at home and abroad, however that will be another story on another occasion.

At this school we had a 'Comprehensive education' which in my opinion, was a sad failure of the British education system at the time. The school and its system was a melting pot of dividing the pupils into 3 main groups: those that were 'no hopers' (called the NF Group), the middle lot and the elite. I was groomed into the middle lot expected to attain an acceptable secondary level of education based on the Comprehensive school model. The elite were children of parents who were well connected and in professions. They always seemed to have the best of things and were delivered to school in cars.

It was the no hopers I felt sorry for as they did not really fit in and most of them were being groomed for life on the farm or in the factories, of which there were many in the nearby towns. Mining, the steel works, the glass works or the BSR who made music centres and turntables. These industries had an annual feed of school leavers who were expected to follow their parents and grandparents into manual labour..

I wasn't and never have been a snob, but for the first time in my life I could see the remnants of the old British class system at work. My own grandparents had been, on my Mothers side, a maid at a country mansion (in the case of my dear old Nan) and a steelworker (for my pigeon fancying Grandad). On Dad's side my lovely Nan was a publican and ran a licenced premises in a nearby town. Grandad, on Dad's side, was a plumber for the local council. My loving Mom worked very hard to bring myself and two younger sisters up as well as holding a part time job in an old folks home (care home today).

My Dad had studied hard after he had finished serving two years in the British army based in Nottingham. That was the reason I was born there. In the beginning he was a trainee accountant and towards the end of his career, a Data Processing Director at a multinational company in Germany. Life had changed for our family and thanks to them the seeds of what I was to become were planted.

I knew then I was different as I was going to be an Astronaut, in fact the UK's first. However the teachers at that school did not believe me!

For now it was going to be that comprehensive school that would be my life for the next 5 years. The teachers that I would get to know, the few friends I would make but not keep, my first girlfriend (who would go on to become my loving wife, and still is over 40 years later!) but above all life outside of the village where I had been brought up, at least during school time anyway.

The buildings at this school were a mix of ancient and modern. It had, in 1970, had a complete renovation with a modern new sports hall built along with a new block with modern centrally heated classrooms and black boards that were built into the wall and rotated on a roller so they had 4 sides to them and plenty of room for the teachers to write upon. They differed so much to the one sided black boards to date, which were mounted upon easels and must have been difficult to write upon with those large pieces of cumbersome chalk.

So, we came to know the building as the 'old block' and the 'new block' The old block looked like any old secondary school up and down the country with its red brick walls and long white painted single glazed wooden windows. Inside these two story buildings were long corridors off which the classrooms could be found. I can still smell the cleaned varnished floors and pinewood to this day and feel the cold drafts on a winters' day wafting down those long corridors..

The new block was just that, a brand spanking new build of a grey breeze block and clad in a stone looking cement, painted beige. The windows were all metal framed and double glazed. The new block class rooms were all so much warmer, I recall, during the colder winter months. The new block also had a kitchen and a dining area, a large lecture theatre (where in Year 3, I would make my acting debut as a white dove in the story of Noah's Ark), a library, and an art room containing a kiln for producing weird clay shapes resembling pots.

Outside the new block, was the sports hall, to the rear of which was sited a 400 meter running track and two full sized football/rugby pitches. These doubled up as cricket fields during the summer season. Beyond all of that was a grassy bank which led down to a nature reserve through which a small stream ran. Many of the pupils went down there to smoke their first cigarettes and/or experience their first kiss!

One final building I had missed was sited between the new and old blocks. It was in fact a new building and looked like a space age laboratory from the outside. This is where the 'new' subject of Rural Science would be taught. The building was a fascinating place complete with stools and high work benches to sit at instead of tables and chairs. It also contained an amazing set of mysterious scientific looking instruments the likes of which I had not yet seen in my short life thus far.

This whole Comprehensive school place seemed to be a living, breathing city after the tiny three class room school in my village. Exciting times of change they were, during the 1970s.

The school pupil count at that time was about 550 children or thereabouts (boys and girls) aged from 11 to 16, plus 12 youths aged 17 in a new sixth form. The pupils were split up into 4 different houses with each house having a name and a colour of either: red, blue, yellow or green. I was to be in the red colour house. Brothers and sisters within the school were kept within the same house. Each house had 6 groups of children which were years 1 to 5 and split up into classes of about 30. The sixth form was different and they had a system whereby they didn't belong to a house except that the Headmaster each year picked a boy and girl each year to be the head boy and head girl of each house so utilising 8 6th formers. I do not know what criteria he used but those children seemed very intelligent and wore the best uniforms, came to school in cars and it did not escape my notice that their parents were all part of the board of school governors.

One thing I will say about almost all of those teachers back then is they were tough but fair. They taught me the foundations in everything I know and planted the seeds in my head of some subjects that I would excel at and in turn some of those same subjects would shape my life. For example, I disliked geography until I met the geography teacher who told me he had spent the last two years in China and of his adventures there. Over the next 5 years, he inspired me and I studied everything possible of physical and natural geography both in and outside of school.

Looking back through my life today, I have seen most of the physical features I studied up close and visited 91 countries and territories in the World even living in and working in 5 of them with my wife and two children. However I did not know anything of that then.

The other teacher who inspired me, but not the subject, was a man who we would call Tapper. Now if you hadn't guessed it he was the woodwork teacher. He had taught my Mom 20 years before and she had told me about him and his reputation. He didn't dress the same as other teachers. He did not look like them either. He mainly taught the children classed as no hopers!. He was a bit like a sergeant major telling people what to do and where to be. He would dress in a check sports jacket and a checked shirt with a red felt tie around his neck. The jacket was clean but well worn with black leather patches sewn onto the elbow parts. He always wore charcoal grey trousers and black brogues on his feet which shone like mirrors. He was always cleanly shaven and had black, combed back 'Brylcreemed' hair with a pointed nose resembling a beak. In fact he reminded me of a barn owl.

In his classroom he always wore a bright white (and highly starched) apron. After the first lesson with him, the class were all told we also needed to wear a white apron in the next lesson and in fact at all times in his classroom. His classroom was immaculate and beautifully clean. He was a man with a very keen sense of attention to detail and this rubbed off onto many of the children, me included.

His classroom was called 'The Woodwork Room' and had work benches within and lots of tools in racks neatly placed in stands around the room. Many of those tools we would get to use in the years ahead. The room smelt of a lovely warm comfortable polished and waxed wood. The lessons were always 45 minutes long, twice a week except a Friday afternoon which was a double lesson and heralded the weekend.

Each lesson would begin by Tapper gathering everyone around his work bench and setting a task for the day. Always, this meant working with a piece of wood of various sizes and practice using a tool. Each term, he would give us a project to work on. For example: the first one was to make an aeroplane from 3 pieces of wood. Once he had shown everyone, he would send you away to your bench instructing everyone to be quiet and concentrate on the task ahead.

Whilst you were working, he would walk around the class and stand behind you to make sure you were doing things correctly. If he spotted anything incorrect he would ask you what you thought you were doing wrong. If you could answer him he would just correct you quietly but if you didn't know he would glare at you and ask you to put your tools down. He would then clap his hands loudly to attract everyone's attention and shout the following instruction: "Right lads, put your tools down and gather round" he spoke with a broad yet educated Black Country accent. Immediately everyone was expected to stop what they were doing, put down the tools they were using and gather around the workbench of the poor child who by now was quivering in their boots.

"Right lads" he would say when everyone was assembled, "can anyone see what he is doing wrong?" Usually, there was no reply as the lads thought if they answered incorrectly they would suffer, in advance, what was coming next. He would then explain the error of your ways and ask you to repeat to the class that you would try harder next time. He would then utter what became known as his trademark catchphrase. He would say "What is he lads?"

Although spoken like a question he did not expect or want anyone to answer and then he would utter his immortal words accompanied with a smack across the top of your head with the top of his right hand "He's a clown, now go back to work the lot of you!"

Everyone would snigger as they thought it funny but God forbid if he heard or saw you do that. The person being chastised would glow bright red in embarrassment as Tapper had 'Clowned' you. That is what it became known as. Within minutes of the next break time, the whole school would know about it and the rest of the day they would call you "a clown". I knew how it felt as it happened to me twice.

Another trick Tapper had, was if you spoke in his class when he had asked you not to. The first time he would shout a warning to the class, "No talking lads, get on with your work" He would already know who it was and importantly, where they were. Often that would be the end of it but there were occasions when the next step was followed. What would happen was so fast and in perfect unison that the receiver would not see or hear anything until it was too late.

Tapper would reach into his left hand pocket, where he kept a black board rubber, and the hand would move this tool so fast from pocket into mid air as fast as a bullet. Once launched it was too late, the projectile would hit the offender somewhere between their chin and belly button! "YOU CLOWN" he would shout. No one dared to move or talk. The room became silent.

I guess today any teacher who did that would be locked up. I have to say I was never on the receiving end of that one, but I think the fear motivation that man instilled is very much needed today. Discipline in an organised and timely manner. It worked, it really did. Some of those lads were very naughty but he turned them! Even now I think back to those times. He gave people a sense of purpose and respect for themselves and others.

Another one of his fine standards that he impressed upon us was cleanliness. I have already mentioned how neat and tidy his classroom was and my goodness it had to stay that way. Many of the lessons involved shaving or sanding wood and so the work benches and floor always would be covered with debris at the end of each lesson.

Now of course, most classrooms got untidy throughout the school but were not cleaned until the end of the day when the children had gone home. However Tapper's classroom was an exception to the rule. No cleaner would dare to enter his domain and he would lock the door when the last class left at 3.45pm sharp at the end of each day.

The reason for this was precisely 10 minutes before the end of your lesson he would clap his hands and shout, "Time to pack up lads". The room would fall silent and every boy then knew his place. Firstly, you would go to a cupboard which contained many dustpans and brushes and select one returning to where you had been working. You then swept the work surface area where you had been working, meticulously, you dared not to miss even a speck of wood dust. You then had to sweep the area of floor around you and then empty the dustpan carefully into a very large bin at the front of the class.

Next, you would return the dustpan and brush to the cupboard being extra careful to put it exactly back where you found it. Then you had to return to your workbench, remove your white apron and fold it neatly and place it carefully in front of you on the workbench. Lastly you would take two steps back and stand straight just checking your school uniform was neat and your tie was straight. All of these tasks were completed within 10 minutes and in an eerie silence.

Tapper would then walk down the rows in the manner of an army officer inspecting his fine troops. Needless to say here, if anything was amiss the clowning ceremony mentioned earlier would be performed and the class would be late going home, especially and unfortuately if it was the Friday afternoon one. He would then select two lads to mop the floor after he had dismissed everyone else. I never discovered his criteria for his selection, however during my time in his 'regiment' I got to mop on 7 occasions.

He knew who the really naughty boys were and he punished them by making them work their break times. Apart from lunch, there were two 15 minutes breaks each day. Tapper ran a tuck shop selling cold drinks, crisps and chocolate. The profits from this went to charity. He got the naughty lads, or those where he was trying to go above and beyond usual teaching, to work their break time serving in the tuck shop. They handled money and were responsible for being accountable. They got rewarded for their toils by Tapper inviting them to select a packet of crisps or bar of chocolate, at the end of their 15 minute shift..

He oversaw the whole operation giving up his own break times tirelessly to teach a sense of responsibility and belonging. Many of the kids (I say kids because some of the girls in that school had broken certain rules too) owe a great gratitude to this man myself included. Apparently he went on to live to a great age and only passed away in 2016.

Whilst still at school, my first job at the age of 13 was not an astronaut. A local farmer had decided that growing crops and milking cows wasn't for him and his family after many generations of his family doing just that. He decided to turn his entire estate (three large fields, a brook and surrounding woodlands) into a golf course. The bulldozers moved in and digging commenced. It was to be a large undertaking in the local community. I was offered the job of chief groundsman (well that's what he described it as). Now that involved recruiting 3 of my most trusted schoolmates and reporting for duty at the development site every Saturday at 7.30am. The task allotted was to go down on hands and knees and pick up any stones and put them in a bucket. When the bucket was full, it had to be emptied into the back of a trailer and you returned to your spot to fill another bucket. I have to say this was boring and back-breaking work but I knew budding astronauts had to start somewhere.

My two loyal trusted mates never showed up the following Saturday so it was just me, myself and I. I have to say for the next 2 years come rain or shine I turned out as requested all bright eyed and bushy tailed.

The effects of this were two fold: firstly, I could actually see the fruits of my labour taking place as the grass replaced the sandy soil and the stones were fast disappearing from the landscape. Secondly, at the end of my Saturday I was handed what would have been a crisp ten bob note but now had become a shiny 50 new pence coin. On a Monday after school, that 50p got taken to the post office and handed over to the postmistress with my Post Office Savings Book.

Another source of income for the Post Office Savings account, was obtained every Sunday morning after I had attended the morning service at St John's Church of England church in the village. Most of the village attended, which I came to realise later was not because they were religious, but because they got talked about if they did not attend. That church witnessed some scandal I have to say over the years. A subject I will cover on another occasion however.

Anyway, at the end of each service I would cycle a route which covered 48 different houses in 3 different villages. I was assigned to deliver raffle tickets for a local charity and collect the money from the sale of them.

A man would deliver the 48 tickets to my parents house on a Monday evening at 7pm prompt. I had to get them delivered and also collect the 20 new pence for the sale of each ticket. When the man called he would collect the cash and the stubs of the tickets to be entered in the following weeks draw. Although not called one at the time, it was all a bit of a lottery. As a side note the man's daytime job was that of an accountant and his name appropriately was Mr Counter.

The draw for the winning number also got printed in the local newspaper and the church magazine. The tickets were sold throughout the county, not just my patch. My compensation for the Sunday morning 4 hour jaunts was 5% of the takings. Now for those mathematicians this amounted to the grand sum of 48 new pence. However there was more, if anyone won a prize I would receive 10% of the prize money and have to deliver their cash. A trusted position indeed for a young lad.

During my time in this employment (3 years and 2 months), I had 3 prize winners. However as the jackpot prize was only £100 I was not going to be a millionaire doing this. My three winners had all made £20 each so the grand total for me was £6 over the time.

Over time I became able to work smart not hard. I did not fancy all those miles ridden for 4 hours so I would hand out the tickets and collect the funds outside the church as people left (with the vicars permission of course). This meant I only had two houses to call on whose occupants did not attend the church and so became the village's most talked about people!

Life was so busy for me back then earning money for my hobby of, well, earning money, saving and seeing the toils of my labour come to fruition. Training to be an astronaut was expensive, you know. I often think back to those days when I drive past that golf club today with its neatly manicured greens and expensive cars parked outside. The farmer died years ago but I can say that his descendants appear to live a most comfortable life.

During my time at the Comprehensive school there was another major event that occurred. It was serious but I did not see it as such as a child growing up. It was a series of measures introduced by the Government to reduce the consumption of energy.

The details, which I did not fully understand at the time, was, a crisis started in October 1973 when Arabic states launched a surprise attack on Israel. The war in the Middle East (as it became known) quadrupled oil prices. Arabic countries reduced supplies to the West. With the price of coal rising too and stocks dwindling, Britain's miners rejected a pay increase and voted to ballot for a national strike.

On November 12, the miners and electricity workers began an overtime ban. I knew from listening to my parents something bad was going to happen but I was a child and too excited about it all to worry. Besides, rumour had it that we would soon have power cuts from 4pm until the next day plunging the country into darkness. Great, I thought, candles in my room to read by and dark skies to see the bright stars.

Another rumour was that the school would close from December 1973 until April 1974 as they would have no coal to generate any heating. Both of those rumours were to become reality.

In early December, the government announced a new set of emergency measures including a 50mph speed limit on all roads, a heating limit of 63F (17C) in office and commercial premises and a reduction in street lighting.

Britons had to get used to living under candlelight as power cuts became a feature of everyday life. For many, it was like wartime Britain again but without the German bombs. As was the case in the Blitz, people rose splendidly to the occasion and adapted well to the new realities.

For me it meant no more school, or so I thought. However the Government brought out a whole new set of rules, one of which was that of school work at home. Much like what is happening at the time of my writing, within the confines of the Covid19 epidemic.

Every Wednesday at 9am we had to attend school for two hours. The instruction was that the school bus would pick us up and transport us to and from school. We were told to wrap up warm as the school was not heated. Also to bring a large bag. We had to attend our usual form class and the form teacher would explain everything.

This was to become the new normal for the next 4 months. Each teacher of every subject would enter the form room and hand out work that they wanted us to complete at home and bring back to the class the following Wednesday. Obviously sports, woodwork and practical subjects were excluded. The deadline and expectations were set and we were dismissed to find our way back to the warm school bus which would transport us home.

Arriving home from school by 12.30 pm to have lunch at home was a real novelty. Ironically, it was probably the first time in my life I felt under pressure though, having to work to tight deadlines. However that pressure soon waned as you got used to the system and by the end of January you could complete the school work within 3 hours leaving the rest of the day to play. This was all before the advent of computers, Google, Skype, Zoom and Google meetings.

It was later that year I bought my first vinyl record (a 45). Dad had purchased a Sanyo music centre and I wanted to copy him by buying records of my own. Only I wasn't interested in his sort of music. I mean who is interested in Bach, Beethoven, Elgar and Mahler (his favorites)? Well not at that age anyway. I needed proper music; black soul music! So it was in Woolworths in Ludlow for 30 new pence I purchased the fine song on black vinyl; 'Lady Marmalade' by Labelle.

Like many things that happened in my life something poignant happened on that day. I did not go to Ludlow with the intention of buying that record or indeed any record. The reason for being in Ludlow was on a school day trip through my English literature class. We were studying Shakespeare at the time, more particular 'Midsummer Night's Dream'.

Now Ludlow Castle back then used to stage a Shakespeare event every year and that year was indeed the Bard's said work. I did not go for that though. I wanted to go for one reason and one reason only. That of Bernard Breslaw!!! Well Berard Breslaw's Bottom.

I will explain, he is the chap who at 6 foot 7inches tall used to appear in many Carry On films. He also had a number of minor British chart hits with his comedic voice. Now, he was going to play the character of Bottom as you may have already guessed. So to see a famous person was my goal and also to go backstage and obtain his autograph.

I never got to see the stage play but I did get to meet Mr Breslaw. I had gone into Woolworths (the one that was in Castle Street, Ludlow) to buy some pick 'n' mix sweets and as I was picking and mixing, this massive figure loomed above me. I turned to see what was blocking out the light. My God! It was him. To cut a long story short here, he was stocking up with the said candy as he said he munched on it backstage to steady his nerves. Amazingly, I was actually talking to him. He was a lovely chap and when I asked for his autograph he duly obliged. Not only that he paid for my pick and mix too.

He had already asked if I was going to see the play to which I answered yes. I thanked him for the sweets and he strode out of the doorway. On my way out of the store I noticed the record counter. In those days behind the counter there was the popular music chart pinned to the wall for all to see the latest 'hits'. This listed the top 30 best selling songs for that week. So I spent the money I had saved on the pick 'n' mix (courtesy of Bernard) on my first ever 45 vinyl record. I never got to see Bernard's Bottom. Just couldn't abide Shakespeare.

In 1975, I applied for and was successful in gaining employment as a 'fish and chicken manager' at a grocery store in the nearest small town. This meant early mornings during Saturdays and school holidays and the attractive financial package would replace my 'lost' income at the golf club as that project had been completed. My cycle was to be dusted down and again put to good use as it was a 45 minute ride in each direction.

I am not sure what the employment law was then or indeed if there was one for a 15 year old working unattended. The job was not quite as advertised and the word manager was incorrect as I was the only person working in that part of the shop, hidden from view. Indeed hidden from view for a very good reason.

The area I was set to work in resembled a small kitchen. It had a long wooden table with a wooden block upon it sited in the middle of the room. There was a double drainer sink with a large brass tap which could be swiveled to run in either of the two porcelain sinks. Above the sinks, was a long rack containing a large collection of very sharp and various sized knives.

To the left was a large window up high on the far wall which was so high you could not see out of it. I worked out that this would be the back of the shops facing a car park as I could hear the sound of car engines. I think it was there just to let in some natural light.

The lighting in the room was very bright and indeed lit up the wooden table resembling a snooker hall. But this was no snooker hall; it was a theatre and not one of dreams but of nightmares.

Above the only door which led into the shop was a hook which I had been told to hang my coat on and to place the white apron which would be found each day hung upon that hook. The man who told me that entered the room, he reminded me of Aker Bilk, the clarinetist, complete with bowler hat on his head, a pointy beard on his face and wearing braces which stood out against his bright bry nylon white shirt. But this man was no musician.

He explained all the 'rules' of his business and how I must be in that room by 8.30am sharp and not to leave until 5.30pm together with the rest of the staff. On no account was I to enter through the connecting door into the shop during those hours except I may pass through as quickly as possible between 12 noon and 12.30pm as long as I was not wearing my apron or carrying any tools of the trade I was soon going to be introduced to.

"Right to work" said the man resembling Aker Bilk explaining what each of the knives in the aforementioned rack were to be used for. The last knife was the most scary, it was enormous, well to me anyway. It resembled half a sword but with a very thick and wide blade. "This one is for chopping" he explained as he lifted it down from the rack, raising it, smashing it down on the chopping block in the middle of the table and looking at me with a big grin on his face. At the same instant his bowler hat fell from his head to the floor revealing his bald sweaty head. "God," I thought, "I didn't know clarinetists could be so scary!"

"Chickens and fish" he explained "but only fish on a Thursday to prepare for Friday." My introduction then to his rules and regulations must have lasted for about 20 minutes and ended with him showing me how to clean all of the knives and place them back in the rack at the end of the day. A pointless exercise I thought as they were already clean at that point.

The 20 minute induction course ended abruptly as a lound bump was heard from outside the building. "That'll be it then lad," said Aker, "your days work." He then opened a large white curtain covering a doorway to the rear of the property. I must say I hadn't noticed this as it was white and blended in with the white walls of this workhouse. He drew back the curtain which made a creaking noise as the metal hooks securing it to a large iron rod were drawn back to reveal a large gauze curtain.

"Now during the day," he explained, "you must keep this curtain closed lad as it keeps out the insects". He then drew back the curtain and thrust open a large iron door revealing a doorway through which the sunlight streamed in at once to fill the room with a bright eerie hue. "Come here lad," he beckoned and I obeyed moving forward towards the doorway. I could now see the full layout of what was to be my workplace for the next 2 years and a routine I quickly had to get used to.

Outside the door there had been stacked 8 large, cardboard boxes, they looked heavy. He helped me lift the first one into the room (well we sort of dragged it between us). "Now lad," he said "I will only show you this once as I need to go into the shop now". He opened the box to reveal its grisly contents.

It was the smell that hit me first, filling my nostrils with a deathly stench which even today I can still recall when I enter my own kitchen to prepare food. In fact, each box contained 50 dead chickens. Their feathers had been removed and they lay there stacked in their dead,naked, spotty flesh, motionless. He put his hand inside the box and selected the first bird. Then, with the precision of a medieval executioner (and what seemed like seconds) he chopped off it's head with the big sword-like knife.

The thud may me jump as the long neck came off. I couldn't believe how long a chicken's neck was. "Right" he said making two incisions at the other end of the body, "you now pull out all of its insides and then you get his neck here and stick it up its arse! Lastly, you then get the bird, swill under one of them taps and put it into that mesh container." I hadn't noticed someone from the shop must have brought that into the room whilst we were pulling in box number 1 of 8.

He went on to explain, when the mesh container was full that I had to ring a little bell, again I hadn't noticed that either. This was a small button sited just below the hook mentioned earlier, sited upon the door. "'Someone from the shop will come and take that away and you can do the next box and so on. RIGHT LAD!" he balled clapping his hands and with a wry smile on his beardy face, turned and disappeared into his shop.

It is at this point that I know it is another one of those times in your life that you will remember vividly forever. The smells, the noises, the cold early morning starts and yes all those dead bodies! How else is a budding astronaut to get on in life without these new skills?

The first week in this job was very stressful, settling into a regime and work pattern. Being quick enough to deal and dissect all that food ready for the table. I haven't even mentioned all the fish but, that again, is a story for another day. The sights and smells and making sure I left at the end of each day with all my fingers and other body parts intact. I still don't know how I achieved all that at such an early age. I suppose in today's modern techno age that it wouldn't legally be allowed.

What I can say is that by the end of the following Summer of 1976 I had the grand sum of £35.37 in my Post Office savings account earning the heady heights of 8.5%pa interest. That was a lot of money to me back then and all from my own labours.

Back then, I filled in any spare time I had by fishing in the local canal. To do this, apart from having some basic equipment, you had to have a fishing licence. This was 35p a year available in the next village from a fishing tackle shop and I was told to carry it at all times whilst fishing as the water bailiff would catch me if I didn't. I never saw such a creature in all that time but imagined him or her as some scaly creature that would swim up the canal when you weren't looking and eat you if you had not got that piece of card in your pocket.

Apart from the associated costs of fishing in the local canal, my lifestyle was very cost effective as Mom and Dad funded most of my daily needs as part of the family.

My other hobby at the time was astronomy due to the fact Mom and Dad bought me a telescope the previous Christmas together with 'The Observer's Book of Astronomy' by Patrick Moore. I became fascinated in the subject and immersed myself in anything I could read on the subject. After all, this would be useful to navigate around the galaxies in my future space employment! During that summer (the one of 1976) I decided to go on holiday by myself. This was to be the hottest and driest summer on record in the 20th Century and many people still often refer to it.

For me I had left school and had from May to September free before I started to attend the college in the nearest big town to study for a HND in business studies. I strapped a tent to the back of my bicycle together with a sleeping bag (both given to me as presents for my 16th birthday) I folded my telescope and somehow managed to place it into a very large rucksack. Then I tied my fishing rod onto the crossbar. I filled a drinking bottle with Quosh orange juice diluted with tap water, said goodbye to Mom and Dad and ventured off on my trusted steed out into the wild blue yonder.

Five minutes later, I arrived at my destination and holiday place for a stay of 4 months. Yes, the field next to the canal and woodland at the back of our house. This venue was great for a number of reasons. Firstly, it was far enough away to be alone. Secondly there was no light pollution from any street lighting so I could do my night time observations in complete darkness. Thirdly I could fish whenever I wished even at night. Fourthly the wood with the cave mentioned earlier were all within walking distance. Fifthly (and most importantly) I could return home for all my meals and ablutions. Life was sweet and it didn't get much better than this.

At this time, I developed an avid interest in anomalous activity although I did not know what that word meant at the time. Basically, in the early 1970s I became interested in 'things that go bump in the night'. Now although all of that stuff borders on scientific research and the stuff of cranks I was so keen on the subject of UFOs and ghosts, that I joined as a student member of 'The Society for Psychical Research (SPR).' Now before you put this book down, I am not going to say much about this subject here as it has been written about many times over by others. However as it did feature as a memorable part of my life I would just like to reference something that occurred in my life at the time.

It all started when I thought I saw a ghost in the village churchyard where I tended to roam from my tent on moonlit nights. This wasn't some weird event but just I couldn't sleep some nights and wanted to go and talk to my Grandad , who was buried there. I wasn't frightened but I knew what I had seen. I thought I would speak to the man who would know about such things, so I cycled to see the vicar at his vicarage in the village. I asked the vicar for the Bishop of Lichfield's telephone number. Puzzled by this strange request he duly obliged. This sticks out in my memory as I thought this would be the first time in my life I would speak to a VIP (in my mind anyway). It was the first time I was to use a telephone. The little red box outside the village post office would be my office for 10 minutes anyway.

I plucked up the courage and opened the door to the little red phone box. This was sited just down the lane where we lived, outside of the post office. A sweet but musty smell entered my nostrils although I could also smell the faint whiff of cigarettes and stale tobacco. That was probably the local youths who would frequent that area after dark. The door closed behind me sealing me inside this sheltered red cubicle.

I had two, shiny, 10 new pence coins in my pocket and could just about reach the receiver which was high above on its cradle. I picked this up and instantly heard the dialing tone. Not a purr back then but more of a continuous single pitched whir. I had already remembered the Bishop's number as I must have looked at it a 100 or more times before plucking up the courage to do what followed.

I dialed the number on the reassuring heavy dial, which whirled and clicked after each number returning back to its original place so you could begin to dial the next digit. There was a brief silence in the ear piece and then the ringing signal.

After 5 rings, a well spoken man answered but almost immediately the noise from the ear piece cut off the voice and I heard a series of rapid pips. I pressed the first coin into the slot marked 10p, it hurt my soft thumb as the pressure required to push it in was very stiff. As I heard the coin drop down through the slot and into the body of the black coated box, the same man spoke again. I identified myself as David and then stopped as my well rehearsed introduction of how to address him stalled. I mean what do you call a bishop? This was the Right Reverend Stretton Reeve, Bishop of Lichfield, but by the time I would have said all that I am sure I would have had to spend another 10 new pence. So I took the easy route and addressed him 'Sir'

He was a most charming man and put me at ease immediately. He assured me he knew who I was as the vicar had already mentioned I would be calling him. But, as he had no idea of why I was calling him, he asked how he may assist me. So I came straight out with it really: "Do ghosts exist and have you ever performed an exorcism?"

He gave a small cough before explaining it was a subject he had not been asked about before. He went on to say it was something he thought would best be dealt with face to face next Thursday when he would be visiting the vicar. "Could I be there at 7pm?" he asked. "Yes mi lord, sorry Sir" I replied and so we bid our goodbyes as a series of rapid pips sounded reminding me I needed to spend another 10 new pence. However back then if you didn't put in another coin you still had about 20 seconds once the rapid pips stopped sounding which was ample time to thank him for talking to me and confirming I would be looking forward to meeting him.

That was a time in my life where I felt really good and positive about doing something. The inquisitive part of me was starting to be developed and the meeting on the following Thursday would prove fruitful and kick start a future life for me when I would use the telephone to call anyone without fear. It was to herald many a meeting with VIPs, the great and the good, people at the top of what they did including famous actors, actresses, presidents of foreign lands that at the time I had never heard of and yes The Right Reverend Streeton Reeve, Bishop of Lichfield.

The meeting with the Bishop took place as we had arranged, together with tea and biscuits, in the drawing room at the Vicarage. However the Bishop asked the vicar if he and I could have this meeting alone. "Wow," I thought to myself I am sat with a real bishop, but you wouldn't recognise that fact without his flowing robes as he had chosen to wear a grey suit complete with dog collar, although the vicar wore a black shirt with his white collar whilst the Bishop wore a maroon red shirt with his.

The Bishop sat in a large armchair by the window and beckoned me to sit opposite him. I did so and as I did he looked across at me and said, "now them young man about ghosts and exorcisms."

Two hours, three more cups of tea and a packet of McVitie's digestive biscuits later (all ushered in by the kind vicar's wife during the course of events), he had explained all about the Holy Trinity and the connection between Father, Son and Holy ghost. I think I understood it all and the meaning of the 3 persons being distinct and yet are one substance, essence or nature. In that context, nature is what one is, whereas a person is who one is.

On the subject of exorcisms, he explained that there were more things in heaven and earth that even he didn't understand. Although he had never performed exorcisms they did exist and he knew people in the clergy who had performed them. In his role of Bishop, he had in his time received two such requests from vicars to perform them both of which he had granted. He went on to explain that Anglican vicars cannot perform an exorcism without a Bishop's permission and to approve such a request he had to consult with a team of specialists including a psychiatrist and a doctor.

"The rest of the subject is 'off limits' to such a young man as you", he said as he rose out of his arm chair. I think that meant the end of the meeting and about all I was going to glean on this occasion. I thanked him very much for taking the time and trouble to speak with me. He thanked me for attending and told me he had very enjoyed us meeting and talking.

As our evening drew to a close he reached down into a briefcase. I must say I hadn't noticed this when entering the room some two hours earlier. He took out a black leather bound book with a gold coloured cross etched onto the front cover. He explained he wanted me to keep this and read it carefully. He opened the front cover of the book and signed his name and date of the meeting, 15 July 1976. He passed the book to me and gestured, advising me to carry it always as protection against any bad ghosts. I once again thanked him and left the room, clutching the book close to my chest.

The vicar was waiting for me by the front door to the vicarage. He too thanked me for coming over. He told me to be careful going home and to leave the bicycle I had arrived on at the vicarage as it was dusk now and I did not have any lights. I obeyed him and thanked him very much before turning and following the little path down from the front door and out into the lane. I clutched the black book and couldn't wait to get home to tell my parents of my meeting and to open that book.

As a note here, some 45 years after that meeting I still have that book. It is a bit dog-eared now as it has been very well read and accompanied me all over the world wherever I have been.

At about the same time in my life, I heard a story from one of the men in the village which I will call the 'Malvern UFO'. This chap used to attend all the church services and was in fact one of the two church wardens. He was an unassuming character who pretty much kept himself to himself. He was married and at the then age of 61, he and his wife had never been blessed with any children.

They lived in a small bungalow in the centre of the village. They were comparative newcomers to the village which was a rarity in itself as most of the residents could trace their relatives back 150 years or more. Indeed the then vicar had been the same man for 41 years at that point.

Anyway back to his story. Firstly, I must say he was not the sort of man to tell strange tales without the whole truth and secondly, I was privileged for him to talk to me as usually he would just just bid people a good morning or afternoon and never engage in conversation.

On this rainy Sunday in August where the rain was so heavy it prevented most of the congregation leaving the church for an hour or so, I sat at the back of the church next to him on a pew. Just the two of us. I just happened to speak to him about the weather to which he replied he had seen much worse than this in his time.

Stuck for more to discuss, I casually asked him if he had experienced any odd things in his time? He then went on to tell me, Five years before he had moved to our village he lived with his wife on the outskirts of Malvern in Worcestershire. He went on to explain that he was ill at the time recovering from a chest infection and that he was laid in bed. On the day in question, he was awoken by a strange 'whirring' noise from outside in his garden. He fully awoke and realised his wife was not next to him in the bed. That was nothing unusual however, as she usually awoke early and made two mugs of tea and brought them back to bed where they would chat before getting up.

Twenty minutes later, she had not returned and by now he was wide awake. He could still hear the whirring noise but now that was accompanied by his dog barking. He got out of bed and looked through the window. He had already explained that their bedroom was to the rear of the house. He recalled that immediately he saw a silver glowing disc like object pulsating and with lights coloured blue, green and red intermittently flashing. This was hovering about 12 feet above his lawn.

He added that he could see a window on the side of this object with what looked like a man wearing a white polo neck jumper. He described this man as Nordic in appearance with blond hair and blue eyes. That is how close he explained that this object was.

From underneath this craft (which he said was still hovering but now lower above his lawn) a silver coloured ladder was lowered and to the left he saw his wife walking towards this. His dog was barking frantically at this sight and ran towards the ladder. As it did so, the ladder seemed to shoot up into the craft as if retracted and the dog with it. The object then spun once on its access and seemed to fold up shooting at immense speed and disappearing into a white dot in the sky.

His wife looked up at him from her position on the lawn and was in total shock. He ran down to her and comforted her. Both of them could not believe what they had seen. He told me they did not know what to do. They never saw the dog again and assumed it had been taken by whatever they had witnessed.

Being in trauma at what they had both experienced, they decided to remain silent on this story and until this point he said they had not told anyone. He made me promise that I would not tell anyone and in my life to this point I have not.

As these people are now both deceased, I am sure they would not mind me retelling this recollection. I have not quoted their names or the exact place or any times or dates.

Whatever happened that day was enough to make them sell their house and move 40 miles away to 'my' village. I have since that time spoken to many people who claim to have witnessed such events but they always had a reliable explanation except for this one. At the time, there was no Google but recently as I write these recollections I have checked and indeed this incident (the sighting of the UFO not anything else)was reported both in the local press and the local TV channel at the time ( ATV Midlands). I have decided to retell this event as it did feature as a part of my life at the time and really made me think more laterally about life in general.

Like most of the times in my life when I have been very content (which is most of it actually), that summertime passed in an instant. The next chapter in my life would soon begin at business college in September 1976.

## **Fit 3 : Becoming a Young Man**

September 9th 1976 was another poignant day for me as I started my first day at business college. This was momentous for me for a number of reasons, one of which was, taking 2 buses and a 45 minute walk so meaning nearly 2 hours travelling time in each direction. I realised that first day I was no longer a child. The world would now see me differently.

Gone was the school uniform and now on with a new, dark navy blue Marks and Spencer suit together with a white shirt and navy blue coat. Dad let me borrow his beige Macintosh to keep the cold out whilst walking to the bus stop and back. So, clad in those clothes clutching an executive looking briefcase, containing my sandwiches for that day, I set out for what was to be the next 44 years of looking very much the stereotypical businessman.

No more being addressed as boy, lad, Dave or David but now Mr Hughes. At college the teachers were called lecturers and were all well dressed. I would now be studying double entry book keeping, law, commerce, industrial relations and computers (yes computers for the first time in my life).

The reason for attending this college was that the headmaster at the comprehensive would not let me stay on into the sixth form as he felt my qualifications were not up to standard. The real reason I suspected was that my parents were not on the board of governors and I lived in another village. My Father appealed his decision as I had achieved the 4 O'levels (in fact I had attained 5, one more than that required to stay on and study A levels in the 6th form) but to no avail. Most of the people I called friends were to leave school and work in the nearby factories and copy what their parents and their parents' parents had done before them. So for this budding wanna be astronaut it was to be the college for now.

Life at college was very sterile for me. It passed quickly, probably because I was so busy studying and making sure I passed all of the exams the following May. During that time, I still maintained my financial independence by working on a Saturday in the shop. I had stopped the raffle ticket deliveries and also stopped attending church on a Sunday as I was simply too busy with college work projects.

During my one year at college I completed my HND in business studies and added two more O Levels which would all look good on my c.v.

Most of the people I knew were already in their employment at various local factories, mainly in the glass industries, that surrounded where we now lived. I saw them sometimes whilst travelling to or from college. They were wearing better clothes than me and talking of going out to the cinema or night clubs. Sometimes, I felt sad as I thought I should be enjoying life and not having to study and be a 'poor' student. But my dad had explained if I kept my nose clean (as he put it) and did what I was supposed to do when I was supposed to do it, the time would come when I could do the things I wanted to do when I wanted to do them. These were to be very wise words looking back, although it didn't feel so good at the time.

It was to be the March of the following year when my life would be changed forever. Well as regards the way I got around. Up until now, I had relied on walking, my trusty old bike, the school bus, the county buses and my Dad's generosity (his cars got progressively more exotic as he was very successful in his career by now). Most of the people I knew had already purchased or were buying their first moped. You could ride one of those death traps on a provisional driving licence, which in the UK at the time was available from age 16. Many of the lads I knew had one and most had suffered some form of accident with 3 months of buying one. They were death traps because although they only had a 49cc engine capacity, from the age of 16 you could just go straight out on the road with no test or anything, except a provisional driving licence. Of course you were not allowed to carry a passenger (although many did) and to ride anything larger than 49cc you did need to pass the motorcycle test. However this was so easy to pass and once passed you could carry passengers and ride a motorcycle of any engine size, in fact beasts which were capable of going faster than 200 mph.

The death toll and serious injuries for motorcycle accidents were rife back then. However they had been reduced from the 50's and 60's as the motorcycle test was, by now, a little more stricter and it was compulsory to wear a crash helmet.

Many motorcycles up until the 1960s had been made in Britain but by the 1970s the Japanese had started to sell motorbikes to the UK that were more sophisticated, cheaper and very reliable.

Back to March 1977, the following year after I started college. After 6 months of me constantly whining about having one, my Dad agreed I could buy my first motorcycle. The provisos were I paid for it myself, looked after it and passed the motorcycle test AND the advanced RAC test.

I looked at many in the local motorcycle shop. In March, I also enrolled on the RAC advanced motorcycle course which involved one night a week travelling to another town (by bus) and a Sunday morning in that same town on the top floor of a multi storey car park. I did not, however, have the motorcycle yet and was the only one in attendance who did not. That was not so important on Wednesday evening as that was in a classroom learning the theory and rules of the road. The Sunday mornings were actually riding a machine on the top floor of the multi storey car park that was closed off for this purpose. I was, however, allowed to use the instructor's machine and felt so honored.

It is at this point I need to thank my Dad very much because his insistence definitely saved me from serious injury or even death. As I sit here, 44 years and 8 motorcycles later, I have never even had so much of a scrape on a motorcycle mainly down to being properly educated and trained at that time. That includes riding motorcycles of all sizes all over the world. Thankfully, nowadays to drive a motorcycle legally in the UK you have to sit and pass a theory and practical test. The reduction in serious road injuries and deaths on motorcycles has been drastically reduced because of this, in my opinion.

Well I am pleased to say that I passed my advanced RAC test just after my 17th birthday and this was soon followed by easily passing the less onerous Government test 3 weeks later. In the July of 1977, I went and ordered a brand new Suzuki B120 registration number VHA490S, in bright red. The total cost was £750 including tax and the first year's comprehensive insurance. I was allowed to take a sneaky peek at it, but what? When they took me into the workshop at the back of the motorcycle shop all I got to see was a large wooden crate.

"That's it" the salesman said. "Come back in a week and it will all be road ready for you". I did not realise when they were shipped from Japan that they were not yet a motorcycle, just a box of bits. The salesman explained they took 9 weeks to go from Japan to the UK packed inside a container on a large ship as that was the best and safest way of transporting them. The shop's mechanic would assemble the contents of the box, road test it and supply it to me in exactly 7 days' time. Well I can say those 7 days passed very very slowly.

Now I did not have £750, only £74.58 in my post office savings account. So at that time not only was my life to change forever as regards transport, but also in the financial part of my life as I borrowed the grand sum of £700 from Forward Trust Loan Company to be paid back monthly at 9%pa interest over 3 years. The balance had been given to me by my Dad as a reward for doing what he had suggested. I can report however that that was all paid back within the next 12 months as both then and now I dislike borrowing money.

Those 7 days did pass and during that time I had been out and purchased a crash helmet and a set of waterproof gloves, trousers and Belstaff waterproof jacket. Items that would be used a lot in the UK's inclement weather. Also items I had to pay for with my newly acquired credit card. This was another financial burden that buying your own transport at an early age entailed. However because I was not yet 18, my Dad had to sign for the credit card and loan which meant although I had the asset of the motorcycle and equipment, he would have the financial burden should I have failed to pay. That did not happen though and I paid off the credit card in full the following month courtesy of the complete contents of my post office saving account.

I was so thrilled when I went to collect my motorcycle and drive it home on the open road. The smell of the leather seat and waft of the oil from the two stroke engine when I started the machine for the first time are all still memorable even now.

Actually, to start it you had to turn a key in the ignition and then swivel out a small lever from down by the right foot and kick this over to start the machine. That was after you had remembered to turn a small key to make petrol flow from the tank and not forgetting operating a manual choke. Left pull on the handlebar clutch lever and left foot to gentle snap it into first gear. Mirror, signal and maneuvering out into a steady stream of traffic and so my life journey of independent travel was to begin. No more waiting for my Dad, hanging around drafty old bus stops or long walks. The world was going to be my oyster and so it would be.

I was a man of the world now. I started to seek employment with my new qualifications complete with my own transport and indeed was successful in finding it at the first application. The local steelworks!

I started to think, what have I gained? Ending up in the steel works where the year before some of my school colleagues now worked. However this was to be different. I had applied for a position in the Transport Department and not on the shop floor. I was to be, what the factory employees called, one of the suits. Yes, it is true I did go out to buy a brand new navy blue pinstripe suit from Moss Bros. I also quickly realised that over the last year and a bit, that they were earning proper money where I had only received a small part time earning from my Saturday job. I had since left the 'chicken gutting trade' for this new position. On speaking to them they revealed they earned a wage paid in cash weekly and I was going to earn a salary paid monthly directly into the bank. When I worked it all out I realised that I was going to be earning double what they were earning but I kept that one quiet. I had already put in the hard labour to be better qualified than them.

My employment position at the steel works was to teach me commercial awareness. I was responsible (being overseen by a transport manager) for making sure the steel made was delivered to the right customer at the right time. I had to book and arrange the transport which was all done then by articulated lorries. I had to ensure the consignment of steel was booked onto the right lorry and sent to the right place. For example one of the biggest customers was British Railways. Not only did they buy steel to make railway engines and carriages, they also purchased steel to make the railway tracks. As such they had depots all over the country and it would be very easy to make a mistake.

This steel works made very good quality steel and as such it had been highly sought after internationally. Customers in as far afield as The USA, Canada, India, The Soviet Union, Malaysia, Hong Kong, China and Taiwan. Many place names I would get to know in all of those far off places, many of which I had to look up in Bartholomew's World Atlas. However my Geography knowledge from school came in useful here too and all of the steel I dealt with in that time got to where it was supposed to and when it was supposed to too.

I did not know it at the time, but years later I would get to visit and indeed live and work in most of those countries, although not with this business. That pleasure (I consider it a privilege) lay in years yet to come.

In May of 1977, I had the opportunity of taking my first proper holiday without parents. I had been in contact with two of my classmates from school over the previous Christmas. They had, by chance, purchased the same Suzuki motorcycles as I had. However theirs were blue machines.

The three of us had spent most of the previous Christmas holiday looking at maps of the UK and planning an adventure. The three amigos! Three young men with a mission. It had to be within a 120 mile range as that was the range of those machines on a full tank of 2 star petrol.

At the time, this to me was a long distance to travel and much much further than the 7 miles from my parents house to work and back each day. We planned it meticulously, the route, the time and the destination into what was going to be one of three visits we would make over the course of the next 12 months.

So the Welsh coast was selected and a little Welsh village near to Barmouth. There was no Sat Nav then just the AA roadmap 1977 edition. It would be a 120 mile trip which meant we would have just 5 miles reserve in the tank on arrival. However, as it turned out, there were more petrol filling stations around back then so in fact we filled up 3 times going and 3 times on the return journey just for safety. We were young and (I guess) a bit paranoid.

The day arrived and all 3 of us stayed at my parents house the night before, not that we got much sleep. In fact, at 4am, we were all so excited about the adventure that lay ahead we got up and dressed. I cooked bacon sandwiches for the 3 of us to eat at two rest stops planned on the way and they were packed away with a thermos flask full of hot tea. All 3 of us had rucksacks packed with enough clothes and provisions between us to last for 7 days.

I opened the front door of my parents house to be greeted by 3 shiny machines packed and ready to go. All had been filled up with petrol the night before and lay pointing in the right direction to Wales. It was a cool and slightly misty late May morning at 4.20am with the expectation that once the sun rose it would be a lovely late spring day. Three young men stepped out into the dawn early morning each sporting Cheshire cat like grins. I had already said "bye" to my parents the night before.

So as not to wake them or anyone else, we pushed our bikes down the drive and out onto the road. Each trusty steed was then mounted and the keys turned in the ignitions and being on top of a hill we pushed off, bump starting them into action half way down the hill.

The journey was amazing, travelling from the edge of English Midlands suburbia, via 4 counties and rolling green countryside which progressively became more mountainous (also wetter and cooler) in appearance. You knew when you had crossed the border into Wales as you could no longer understand the road signs or the writings on the road. Also I have to say when you entered Wales from England a large sign read 'Welcome to Wales' (well actually Croeso y Cymru) with a picture of a red dragon and the Welsh flag. This is more than can be said going in the opposite direction into England which just says Shropshire. However I understand there is nowadays a welcome to England sign with the English flag depicted.

After 4 stops enroute, one for the bacon sandwiches prepared earlier and 3 for fuel, we arrived near Barmouth in a place called Tyddnn Nant. Now even today (when I have learnt to speak 7 different languages one of which is Chinese, to read and write) I still do not know what that means.

We soon found our prebooked, illustrious accommodation, which for the next week was a very small, 3 berth caravan which must have been made in about 1920. I will say more about that in a while. However at this moment what puzzled the 3 of us is why our motorcycles had registered 3 different mileage readings. We had all set the trip counters of the speedometers to zero at my parents house, however mine said we had covered 112 miles, my one friend's 115 miles and the third 116 miles. Sadly, like three blue nylon anorak wearing enthusiasts, the rest of the day's conversation centered around various theories as to why the mileage readings were as they were with no answers provided at all!

Now, back to the accommodation. As mentioned this was a three berth caravan that became known to us as A4. That was the number written upon the door and no reference to paper size. To this day we still laugh about it as it was to become a subject of perverted ridicule and the joyous accommodation of 2 further holidays yet to come. That caravan was our holiday home but sadly it lacked a number of basic amenities. For a start off, it had no running water. That had to be collected in a milk churn from a standpipe the other side of a field. Easy to find as it was besides a toilet block, in fact 'The' only toilet block because that is where you had to go for your ablutions, as caravans then didn't have a toilet. It was like living back at the little cottage when I was younger. But what the heck, this was our home now and our three motorcycles fitted nicely right outside the door to the caravan.

That first night in A4 was odd for another reason. It only had one bed. A double one that pulled out of a wardrobe on the wall. So the three of us had to sleep on it as best we could. Sleep is the wrong word though as we continued to discuss the discrepancies with the actual mileage we had covered that day. Thinking back, it was all so cosy and normal but today three men in one bed would get you talked about, I am sure.

The following morning arrived so quickly, and as I was the self-appointed chef (only because that meant one of the other two would wash up) I shot into action in the kitchen on the two ring Calor gas oven, complete with a small grill. Never mind I cooked up some fine cuisine, on that little beauty.

I did not like the wildlife in the kitchen: three large spiders in the drawer containing the cutlery, a dead mouse in the saucepan cupboard and woodlice around the sink. But hey up, we were 3 lads on an adventure.

After breakfast, whilst my 'staff' attended to the washing up and slaying the kitchen wildlife, I walked across the dew laden grass to the toilet block. Words like unspeakable do not even get close to describing this little brick building with one side for ladies and one side for men. You could easily find this place by following the acrid smells emanating from within.

Inside, there were three cubicles: one was always marked 'out of order' with the door nailed shut, one was a filthy and most disgusting toilet and the other was a shower. Inside the shower, mounted flimsily high on a wall, was a coin operated meter. Presumably that was to activate the hot shower if you were to insert a 10p coin and turn a metal dial. I never found that out though as I did not want to put my health at risk by exposing myself in there.

The rest of the week, my bathing would take place in the sea and I would use the public toilets in Barmouth for my bodily functions. Only first thing in the morning and last thing at night, would I use the toilet part and only if desperate. By the end of that week though, there was no chance of getting anywhere near the toilet as there was a constant queue of people waiting. Reason being that it was the Whitsun Bank Holiday and many people had descended onto this hell hole. Still happy memories! My future wife and I would return to this place 3 years later for a laugh. Though on that occasion we did not stay in A4 as we were told it had gone to the knacker's yard. Fortunately the toilet block had been demolished by then and the newer A4 replacement came with all mod cons including: running water, a flushing toilet and a four ring cooker. Bliss.

During my time in the steel works, my childhood sweetheart and I got married in the village where we had met at school.

(The village where she still lived). Gosh we were so young. I was still only 19 years of age and she was 17. Not only that we purchased our first house together. However, the house had to go in my name only as my wife was not yet 18 and so could not go on the title deeds.

Our wedding was a traditional white wedding day complete with the church, choir, bells, bridesmaids and page boy & girl and yes, of course it rained all day long. We held the reception in the local village hall where my wife and I had prepared all of the food and drink. In fact, we arranged and indeed carried off the day by our own careful planning.I don't know how we did all that but it made us grow up so very quickly.

The house we purchased to start off our married life, was in the cheaper part of a small town nearby and was a mid terraced Victorian house, built in 1885. A small but comfortable two up two down little home. Little did I know then that during the coming years we would move a total of 14 times and own a second home abroad. Three of those moves would come after we had children and be as far afield as: France, Singapore, Taiwan and Thailand. But those places never existed in my mind at that time.

In the same year, we married, it became apparent that I could not expect my future wife to travel on the back of a motorcycle in all weathers. The dilemma I had, however, was that I did not know how to drive a car. Back then because I had passed my test on a motorcycle, it also meant you could drive a motorized three wheel vehicle. So enter into my life... the Reliant Robin.

A lot has been said and written about Reliant Robins and not all very nice things. However the advantage was we could sit side by side in the warm and dry whilst travelling and also store the shopping in the back. However the 'Plastic Pig' as they were known as , was simply a horrid beast. Being made of fiberglass they were very light to steer and as they only had three wheels, if you went around a bend in the road too quickly it would be easy to turn over. However I have to say I was very careful to protect my dear wife and that never happened.

The Reliant Robin, wasn't as per the manufacturer's name sake, reliant. It was forever difficult to start in cold weather and constantly breaking down. Every 3,000 miles it had to have a full service. In the snow, it was almost impossible to drive as the front wheel would fit nicely into the rut in the middle of the road making the ride very bumpy indeed and almost impossible to keep straight. Therefore there were many accidents in this type of vehicle.

 Apart from what I have just mentioned you could legally drive them by owning a motorcycle licence. However the configuration was exactly the same as a car inside. It had four seats, a gear stick and a steering wheel. All this felt so strange having been used to 2 wheels. I don't think in the 18 months I owned this contraption I ever exceeded 40 miles per hour. It did however take us all the way to South Wales and back on our Honeymoon. It never broke down once on that trip either, surprisingly.

Everyone remembers the first time they flew in an aeroplane and for me Well, I was no exception. In fact, I remember the second flight too and the third. The third probably more so as that was the first time I actually experienced landing in an aeroplane. Let me explain. The first two experiences were near the village where I grew up. It was an old World War Two military airport that had been decommissioned and now used for light aircraft and also a sport which I took up briefly to raise money for charity. If you have not guessed it, it was parachute jumping. The thought of this now fills me with dread although even then I had sleepless nights worrying about it. However, as a young man still wishing to be an astronaut, I thought this would take me one step closer or indeed could have taken me a step closer to meeting my deceased great grandparents.

Back at this time, as of today, you cannot just go up in an aeroplane and jump out. Unlike today, however, you did actually jump out solo and activate the parachute yourself by pulling a rip chord which would hopefully deploy the chute and support you all the way to the ground. Before all that you had to attend two full days of training with two ex-military paras. At the end of that, if you passed their rigid and strict training, you could apply for membership of the British Parachute Association. This was serious stuff and legally essential. Membership gave you insurance cover in case you crashed through someone's roof or landed on their car.

Total cost of all that plus the training was £300. That was a lot of money back then and came out of my own pocket. Any money I would raise for charity was on top of that. In fact, people thought I was mad at the time as they said it would be far less painful for me to just give the training fee to charity and not do the jump. I mention jump as it was only supposed to be just one jump.

Anyway, as usual I didn't listen to my 'advisers' and so enrolled on the course. This was to be held in one of the old draughty aircraft hangers which, inside had the middle part of an old aeroplane fuselage to practice getting into and crucially out of the craft. Although this was a mock up on the ground, in reality the live jump would take place 6,000 feet above it.

The instructors addressed themselves as Pat and Bob and you could tell they were ex-military. Not interested in small talk or your name, they ordered you what to do. You were not allowed to speak unless spoken to. Both of them were battle hardy as they had just served in the Falklands Conflict in 1982 in the Parachute Regiment on active service. (Although they never talked about this or even mentioned it at the time).

On the first day of training they discussed what a parachute was and took us into the 'Packing Shed' to go through the finer details of the chute and all the working parts. I was shocked as to how big a parachute was and how it would pack into such a small backpack. We were to use the standard Nato military chute made of silk. Next to it, spread out on a bench, was a smaller, white coloured parachute which we were told was a reserve chute in case the first one did not open. This would be strapped to your front.

The afternoon of that first day was concerned with weather and wind speeds and what happened when you exited the aircraft. Apparently, you could not jump if the wind speed was above 20mph and we were directed in the gaze of an orange windsock which was outstretched in the breeze, on the far side of the runway. "Right," one of them said,"that means 30 mph so if it were today, you could not jump". We were shown diagrams of the windsock in different conditions so you could understand the wind speed. The day ended with my mind swimming in aerial facts.

The second day, which took place in the same hanger, was the action part. This was about what to do as you exited the aircraft, what to expect, how to steer the parachute (which I did not know you could), what to do if the thing failed to open and how to land without breaking your leg. It was all scary stuff and I began to realise that the colour of adrenaline is brown.

Later that same day, I could hear the motors of an aeroplane and for the first time we were introduced to the craft that would actually take us up. It came into view at the end of the hanger but we initially were not allowed near it. A two hour talk then followed about walking around the craft without getting limbs cut off by either of the two spinning metal propellers. We were introduced to the pilot. Again, he too was ex-military so we were in good hands.

Later that same day, we were kitted out with the parachutes and instructed on how to enter and exit the twin engined Highlander aircraft. As you approach the aircraft the responsibility for safety passed from the instructors to the pilot. He went through the emergency procedure if in the unlikely event something were to go wrong. Although I must say I felt a lot safer then, than I do these days on a commercial aircraft as I was wearing two parachutes.

The aircraft could take 7 parachutists and one instructor. The instructor did not wear a chute, as space was limited with 7 jumpers wearing equipment, but he would be accompanying us in case someone failed to jump or something went wrong.

There were no seats in the aircraft just a bare fuselage like a freight plane. We were the freight and we were to sit two people facing each other down the fuselage. One of the reasons for this, was for weight distribution to be equal and also only two people could just fit in in succession. Once the aircraft reached 6,000 feet, a green light would glow by the doorway. I had not noticed this on entry or the red light by the side of that. The instructor introduced us to the the lights and we were told red meant stay put and don't move. Only when the light shone green, could you move onto the door ledge ready to jump and sit with your legs dangling over the edge, presumably looking down to view what 6,000 feet looked like from above. When one person was in the doorway, the second would begin to shuffle forwards ready to assume the position. After the first had gone with the green light still shining could the second one jump. Then the red light would ignite and the aircraft would circle the airport again to be back into a similar place to where the first two had exited. The reason for this was to make sure the team all landed in a similar zone down below.

This would continue until you got to jumper number seven. As you may have worked out this 7 is an odd number which meant number seven would be the last jumper and on his own. We were told 'lots' would be drawn on the day to see which position you would be in, the shortest drawn would be number seven and the longest number one with the rest of the order on the differing lengths of the straws.." God! Not 7" I prayed because I would have to watch the others jump first! And also be in full view of the instructor. Speaking of whom, at the end of this session, which was still on the ground, remember, he introduced us to his very sharp and very long knife.

"Now this isn't to chase you out, if you freeze and can't jump, the bottom of my number 9 boot will do that" he laughed. But this was no laughing matter and he held the knife up for everyone to see. "This in case you panic and release your parachute and it gets tangled on the aircraft. It is unlikely but could happen". If it did he explained you would be still attached to the aircraft and towed along 6,000 feet in the air. He would then have to crawl past any remaining jumpers, show you the knife so you knew what was going to happen next. He would then cut through the tangled lines releasing you so you would fall away and use the reserve chute strapped to your chest to survive. I was getting nervous again now.

The final part of that last day involved being shown a diagram of the airport from above and what it would look like from 6,000 feet up in the air looking down. The point of this was essential knowledge. The airport had three runways and they formed a triangle as in fact most do. I never knew that. Once you exited the aircraft, immediately forming a star shape with your body so giving the parachute a perfect platform to deploy from your straight back. You would then shout "ONE THOUSAND, TWO THOUSAND and THREE THOUSAND" (shouting it out aloud as you fell) at this point it was calculated you would have travelled far enough from the aircraft and the following jumper so as not to get tangled. Also, you would now be traveling in freefall at 200 miles per hour and have exactly 15 more seconds before you hit the ground dead. So all in all a complete poop fest.

A metal 'D' shaped ring would be clasped in your hand which you would now pull and almost immediately (in theory) your body would change to an upright position. Next, you had to look above your head to see the full open parachute which should now be a perfect circle, above your head. If you could not see it or it was not a perfect circle you would then look for the second but smaller 'D' shaped ring attached to the pack strapped to your stomach area. This was in fact the reserve shoot. It was estimated if you needed to perform this maneuver you would be now 10 seconds from the ground and would only have just enough space for the second chute to deploy springing from your chest.

Ok, so assuming your main chute had deployed successfully two toggles on nylon white ropes would drop either side of you. If you pulled on these they would take you to the left if you pulled the left one or to the right the other. You were instructed, NEVER to pull both at once or the parachute would begin to oscillate (I never knew what that word meant until that time either) and if you continued to pull them, the parachute would close up like a crumpled handkerchief and you would fall to your death as by now you were nearly on the ground.

Right, that was how you steered your chute. Backwards and forwards was also possible but with everything else thus learned, I had forgotten that one. Only to say the instructor had said not to worry about that as he and the pilot would have worked out up in the sky when you could jump and would have calculated the position of the plane and airspeed to allow for that.

So, with all the aforementioned in mind and as you were suspended there you now had to prepare to steer and land the chute. Again, in theory, this was easy as you simply looked down to find the centre of the runways (ie the 'A' point in the triangle) The instructor had made the forward and backwards calculation and you simply had to look down your leg to your boot and aim for the said point using the toggles to go left or right. As an added backup, the other instructor would be on the ground shouting up instructions through a megaphone. Sadly, as you will see later this added measure to build your confidence was not to happen.

Well that was it, the training was completed. Out of the 24 people who attended that course, 5 were never seen again! They were too frightened to continue. 5 failed the course and that left 14 of us, including me, I had miraculously got through. We were sent home and told to wait 10 working days during which our BPA applications would be processed and a membership card sent out.

Sure enough, that is exactly what happened and with fine military precision I received a letter with my membership card and instructed to report back at the airport at 06.00 hours on 24 July to do the deed (weather permitting of course). That was 7 days from now. OMG!

The following week, I don't think I slept well at all and even when I did I had the strangest of dreams. But eventually 'tempus fugit' and 06.00 hours came. Well in fact 04.00 came first as that was when I woke up absolutely petrified. There was to be no way back now as the sponsorship form had over

500 names upon it due to me knocking every door in this and two neighbouring villages (and also 30 or so relatives). A total of £1032 would be collected if I was successful and it was time to do or die!

That 24 July was another day in my life where I would remember it well and be etched in my memories evermore. The fact I am writing this is verification, to this point, is that I would still be very much in the land of the living by the end of this momentous day. However, it is with sadness, that between the training course and this day, Pat who I had so much respect for had unfortunately been killed in a parachute accident. He was 7th out of the plane the previous Sunday and both of his chutes had failed to open. Really a tragic and sad event. That man along with his partner, Bob had told me everything I now knew about flight and prepared me physically and mentally for the day ahead. He had done over 10,000 jumps and survived active conflict. He would jump from 15,000 feet plus as he was experienced and therefore classed as a skydriver.

His death was sad but in a strange way motivated me to get this job done. I owed it to him and all the people who had sponsored me. I drove my three wheeler to the airport in silence not even switching on the radio, as I usually did from habit. It was a cool summer day and had been light since 4.30am, the sun had already risen and I intended to see it set later that same day. This man had his mission.

The remaining members of the team assembled at 06.00 where we had completed our training. As I parked my Plastic Pig I could see the Highlander aircraft out on the airport apron surrounded by the runway complete with it's rear door open. There was a dew on the grass and an expectancy in the air.

We bid each other a 'good morning' as the surviving instructor, Bob walked in clapping his hands loudly to gain everyone's attention and indicate we should be silent. As if that was needed, as apart from a brief good morning no one spoke. No one was to speak in the next 10 minutes either as Bob gave us the news about Pat's death. I do believe everyone was so pumped up with adrenalin that they had failed to process the information we had just been given.

Bob already had Pat's knife attached to his waist band and reminded us about it if we got into difficulty in the aircraft. Fourteen parachutes and fourteen reserve chutes were visible in the far corner of the hanger. As we drew the lots to see the order of jumping; you would move forward together with the second person and help to strap on each other's chutes. Bob came around each person to double check all the right parts were where they should be and fastened correctly.

I remember I was dressed in a navy blue, nylon Adidas tracksuit which felt comfortable and warm even with so much baggage strapped around my body. However I think I must have looked like a big daddy bumblebee complete with my black Dr Marten boots as I walked forward and was told to sit on the grass. I was to be in the second group of seven and would be number 3 out of the aircraft. The first group walked silently past towards the Highlander aircraft, whose twin engines had now burst into life. They were in a line in jump order with Bob in the lead as he would be first in the aircraft. We knew each person on the lists of jumpers so we could watch for them when they were exiting the aircraft.

Also, out on the grass was a man from the local newspaper who had heard what was happening. Actually he was there to interview Bob about Pat's tragic death and about whether free fall parachute jumping was safe or ought to be banned. He had a camera with a telescopic lens which he agreed (after Bob told him he had no comment to make and would do no interview) to take each and everyone's picture as they left the aircraft. I still have that picture today and it still fills me with mixed emotions wherever I come across it in a drawer.

By now, the first group were all safely inside the aircraft and it slowly taxied towards the runway. The pilot would be testing the controls and radioing the control tower by now. I noticed the rear door was in the open position which was standard back then in case the occupants needed to evacuate the aircraft quickly in an emergency. The Highlander was now in position at the start of the runway. The pilot would now be asking for permission to take off and would be opening the throttle on the engines to full ready to disengage the brakes and accelerate down the runway. The control tower would be saying "permission granted, proceed at your discretion" and the aircraft eased forwards down the runway accelerating to 140 miles per hour before it became detached from the ground.

The noise of the aircraft turned into a distant drone as it slowly climbed to 6,000 feet by circling around the runway 12 times. Higher and higher it climbed. Then it seemed to level out almost directly above us. I looked out across the runway to where the orange windsock was atop a white pole. It was just soggy and limp, an indication virtually no wind today. Perfect jumping conditions.

The man from the newspaper had set up his camera on a tripod and had a massive telescopic lens attached to the front of it. He was looking through the viewfinder. Almost as he did this, the drone of the engines became almost silent, that meant the pilot had cut his engines and would have switched on the green light. Almost immediately you could see a little black dot in the sky and then the orange, green and white shape of a fully open chute followed by another and then you could hear the sound of the engines again as the aircraft turned to circle to get back up to 6,000 feet and deploy the next two. It all happened so quickly and by the time the first parachutist touched down (well crash landed to be more precise) the seventh was already visible in the sky.

However, not all of the first load were to land in the centre of the runway and indeed two of the seven didn't even land inside the airport! The instructor beforehand had pinned an orange disk which was 8 inches across in diameter. He said that you would be able to see this below from 6,000 feet and so 'steer' towards it. For me that was not to happen, as you will see in a while. It certainly wasn't to be for the first two jumpers either.

The first one landed on the hanger roof with a metallic thud, but was thankfully unarmed. The second landed upon the instructor's Landrover Defender and bounced off the roof. The effect of this miscalculation sprained his ankle but didn't harm that fine British vehicle. I thought that they had not listened to the instructor during training, something which I had done and would not be making the same foolish error. I knew what to do. Wrong! More on that is a moment. All of the Jumpers 3 to 7 all landed within the airport grounds but none of them within the triangle. Although I didn't witness jumpers 3 to 7 land as I was with my team walking away from the drop zone and to the opposite end of the runway to where the aircraft was now rapidly approaching ready to fill with it's next load of novices.

Soon it would be my turn and I had never, at that time in my life, been up in an aircraft! The aircraft bounced down onto the runway, went past the 7 of us and turned a sharp 360 degree to approach our position on the grass where we had been told beforehand to wait. The aircraft drew to a stop but with both engines still running. The instructor leaned out of the open rear doorway and beckoned us to approach with his open hand. We had been briefed on his hand signals beforehand.

Gingerly the row of seven moved towards the aircraft in correct jumping order ie. number 7 first downwards to number one last. Each climbed into the doorway, the first being pulled in by the instructor as there were no steps up to the plane. The following jumpers pulled in by the one before them until we were all loaded. We all sat silently opposite each other on the floor of the aircraft as it did not have any seats. We glanced frontwards to the cockpit where the instructor sat opposite jumper number 7 and he made the OK signal to us. Each jumper made the same signal back and he then turned to speak to the pilot.

Where I was sitting, I could hear the drone of the twin engines which suddenly had turned into an ever louder drone as I felt the power surge and the aircraft move forwards. Fast, faster and then faster than I had ever been in my life to date as I looked out of the rear door and saw the ground move below. Slow at first as I could see the blades of grass and daisies on the side of the tarmac and then whoosh and the aircraft started to climb. I felt myself slide backwards almost as if the rear exit had magnets attached to it drawing me to it's jaws. The weight of the person behind me pushed hard against me. I watched as the ground disappeared. I tried to make out distinguishing landmarks as I knew the area below but as I had never seen the area from this perspective I gave up and focused on the task that lay ahead.

I glanced across at the others who were all sat expressionless, my gaze finally falling upon Bob the instructor who looked pensive. I thought he must be missing his flight partner but didn't know anything about what he must be going through in his mind. He must have been 10,000 jumps or more ahead of my simple thoughts.

I counted the circuits that the aircraft would have made now and looked down on a patchwork quilt of fields and woodlands below. We must be at 6,000 feet by nowI thought. Looking horizontally out of the door, the landscape seemed to disappear into a haze. I looked at my wristwatch, which read 2.59pm. Stange how you can remember things like that. I could feel a nervous shuffling and then almost as suddenly the aircraft engine slowed, I knew this was it. The first two jumpers moved towards the open door, the light was on red. The first moved into position legs now hanging over the door sill with his body pointing towards the exit. The instructor was watching him as he raised his hand and made the OK sign, the instructor replied likewise.

At that moment the engines cut and an eerie silence filled the cabin. The light now illuminated green. Number one hesitated and looked to check his position. He moved forward and then disappeared. He had gone. Number two quickly filled the doorwarway and followed him, just as the light changed from green to red. The engines started up again and I could feel the aircraft turn and climb. This was it now, I would be next. I slid quickly to the door looking out. I looked behind me and saw jumper 4 moving behind me, his boot pointing in the direction of my rear end. I knew when it was my turn if I froze in the doorway it would be the bottom of this boot that would assist me in going through into the abyss.

The engines fell silent, I looked at the instructor and made the OK signal. I really felt scared and sick. He raised his hand to reply. I could feel my heart beating and hear it in my head as the red light changed to green. My hand was tightly clasped to the D ring of the ripcord. I looked out into the air and pushed off. The next few seconds were insane. I could feel the cold rush of air. Instead of opening my body into a star shape, I in fact curled up into a tight ball and closed my eyes. I felt helpless. Where the hell am I? Totally disoriented. I pulled the D ring which by now was cutting into my hand. Almost at once I felt as if the air had stopped rushing. I tried to look up to see the perfect circle of the parachute above me. But my God! My head and neck felt locked. I could not move them! I could not look up. I did the next instinctive thing and pulled the ripcord in front of me. I felt a sharp pain as if someone had punched me in the stomach.

Instead of deploying the reserve chute it was now wrapped around my left leg. I thought that must be good as the main shute must have been opened. It actually had but because I was curled up into a tight ball facing downwards the chute had tangled around me but fortunately had now dislodged and as I looked up a second time I could see the reassuring sight of a perfect nylon circle above me. This all happened in a matter of seconds because the next thing that registered was the utter silence. I mean you could not hear a thing. It was heaven. I felt totally at peace for the next few seconds.

I now looked outwards and relaised that I could see the airport. But wait! not where it should be. It should be directly below me but it wasn't. I could see the two toggles that had somehow become untangled and I would now be able to steer left or right. But it was too late for that the ground was becoming ever closer and the airport was now behind me. I had drifted away in my panic and now could see the hedges marking the boundary of the airfield. I could also see a very large house with a very big greenhouse. I must have been about 100 feet off the ground now and totally out of control.

Thankfully I could see I was going to miss the house and more importantly my potential glassy fate. I drifted over two hegrows and could see 4 horses in a field and as all that happened I prepared to hit the ground. We had been taught 'to think banana,' which meant to try and bend into the fall and roll through as you hit the ground. I hit the ground sideways and as I did so, I put into practice what I had been told. The force of hitting the ground wasn't how I thought it would be. It was quite gentle. I made contact and rolled to the side. The horses were startled but I don't think this was their first experience of dealing with wayward parachutists as they briefly looked up and then continued to graze on the lush green grass that had so helped break my landing.

I quickly gathered both silk parachutes and folded them up as best as I could. The strings of the reserve had somehow untangled from my leg. I was still sat on the floor and just started to wiggle everything to make sure it still worked. Then I slowly arose. Yes! All seems to be working. By then I heard shouts from the gate at the far end of the field. It was a fire engine from the airport. They had watched my fall and assumed the worst. They had already called 999 for an ambulance. I felt foolish walking towards the neatly dressed fire officers. They met me by the gate and undid all of the buckles to release all of my equipment. They then placed all of this in the back of the fire engine. They then made me sit in the back of the cabin and checked me over. "No problems" I said and indeed I was absolutely fine and wanted to tell everybody of my experiences. But they had heard it all dozens of times before. They turned off the sirens and blue flashing lights and drove me back to the airport hanger, where by now, embarrassingly, an ambulance was waiting for me..

The Highlandlander aircraft had landed and Bob assembled us all for a debrief. The ambulance was needed but not for me. Jumper number 6 had unfortunately landed awkwardly and needed hospital treatment for a suspected broken leg and jumper 7 needed treatment for shock. He actually failed to jump and had to land with the instructor in the aircraft. Now I was beginning to understand the challenges and dangers of this sport and how within 5 years it would be banned for novices except for tandem jumping where you actually make your first three jumps on the back of your instructor.

Bob got everyone to assemble in the hangar where seats had been put out for those who could still sit. The air was filled with a buzz and everyone was talking enthusiastically about what they had just done. Bob had to clap his hands 5 or 6 times before the room fell silent. He began by congratulating everyone left in the room and explained the fate of those that were not. He went on to say that those present had passed the course and with our first jump completed we could go again in the future. He went on to say that certificates of competence would be sent to us all and because the membership of the BPA was for 12 months we could come back to do other jumps and still be covered by the benefits of the membership.

He looked at his wristwatch and said that we could now be dismissed. Tea and coffee would be served in the cafe underneath the air traffic control tower for those not in a hurry to leave. Then he dropped a bombshell and explained as it was still early in the afternoon and that the pilot still had another two hours of flying time left, that anyone wanting to do a second jump could! Through the back of the hanger I could see the pilot standing as if to attention, still kitted up in his flying suit complete with a hard hat. I must say I had not thanked him up to that point, especially as my life had been completely in his hands that day.

Bob asked for a show of hands from those assembled who would like more torture. Only 3 hands were raised. He explained he would make up the 4th but that he would jump out last after the aircraft had climbed to 15,000 feet. I sat there still processing the request and without further ado gingerly raised my hand.

"'Very good" he grinned "that is the number we need to make this viable and 5 was always my lucky number: lets go!". He shouted as he pointed to the control tower and added "'we meet there in 10 minutes".

Most of us walked to the control tower again with people talking loudly in excited tones, all except those going again who had suddenly gone quiet, including me. When we reached the control tower cafe, Bob was already there and he was starting to don his gear.

On the tables were 4 new and neatly packed parachutes and reserve chutes. I suddenly realised we still had our crash helmets securely fastened to our heads. "Right no tea and cakes yet for those going again!" yelled Bob. He then told us to don the equipment laid out with another person assisting in checking everything. He gave everyone a second check before we followed him down the two flights of stairs and into the back of the waiting Highlander. He had already (on the walk) told us our jump order. I would be 2nd (that has always been my favorite and also my lucky number).

Everything was very much a repeat of the first run except this time when I left the aircraft I was very alert and did a textbook jump. As I came into land I could see the orange disk and in fact landed just 2 feet away from it. "Yes!" I yelled thinking the next flight I would make would be into space. However that wasn't yet to be.

In reality my next flight (first commercial one at least) was some two years later and involved flying to the Far East from London. During that 12 hour flight, I would be sitting next to a very nervous passenger who had asked me if this was my first flight. When I explained it was not, she went on to ask what the landings were like. I smiled inwardly to myself and answered that I did not know as in my previous two flights I have not landed in the aeroplane. That was the end of that conversation.

As I look back at that day, I realise how much I had learnt in such a short space of time. How much respect I now had for the military wherever they are in the world. Brave men and women who would jump into enemy territory to secure an objective, often under fire. That is something that in my life, so far, I have not had to experience as my two jumps were for 'leisure' and entered into voluntarily. As a side note, I had raised money for charity as mentioned earlier and decided to donate all of the proceeds to Cancer Research. I did not know this at the time but that C word would affect so many people I would know including close family members in the years that lay ahead. As such years later the profits from this book will also be donated to the same charity.

I had this strange dream the other night about getting old and all that. When I woke up, I realised that in my life so far I have already outlived both of my Grandads by age and, as I think about the meaning of life, I am also a Grandad three times already. What is age if not just a number though? I mean if we live for three score years and ten (as my old Nan used to say) then I am old but not yet out. It would also mean that middle aged is 35! But is it? Scientifically, it appears that middle aged is anywhere between 35 and 55 and old age doesn't start until 80. So there is hope for us all then. Well that's my thought of the day done. I can go back to changing the channel now with my mobile phone as I have probably left the TV remote in the fridge again.

**Fit 4: Learning Chinese**

Time passes so quickly when you are having fun. It was now 1986 and my wife and I were approaching our 7th wedding anniversary. We had already moved house for the third time and now lived in a large house in the Worcestershire countryside. This was the house in which my wife would become pregnant and give birth to our beautiful two daughters later in 1988 and 1991.

It was about this time that I started reading books on developing a positive mental attitude and indeed attended a number of conferences on the subject. One of the most strongest and poignant phrases to come out of all of that for me. was ' you can have anything you wish as long as you help enough other people get what they want!' I suppose that is the main reason I had moved on from the ailing steel industry and moved into financial services. That enabled me to put into practice what I was studying, helping people to get what they want.

I became involved during the growth years of financial services in advising on investments, pensions, life insurance, wills, trusts and mortgages. This was Margaret Thatcher's Britain. Almost everyone was becoming entrepreneurial. Council house tenants were buying their own houses, the ordinary man in the street was buying up stocks and shares in public utilities that were passed from Government ownership into private hands. It was a growth time. A great time of change across the whole of the UK.

I purchased my first mobile telephone in 1987. It was shaped like a brick and with a battery the size of a lady's handbag; mobile was hardly the right word, more like portable. Back then, there were only two mobile telephone networks. Celnet and Racal-Vodafone. You had to buy the telephone for £1300 including VAT. At the time, you could almost buy a decent second hand car for the same price. But I had to have it as my job involved visiting clients all over the country, either in their own homes or places of work. I needed this invention to stay in touch whilst I was on the move.

You could only really use the telephone at or near town centres or along the major motorways within the UK. Therefore, more often than not, I was still stopping to use the red telephone boxes to keep in touch on my journeys and

15 hour working days. Yes, times had changed and you really could have anything you wanted if you helped enough other people get what they wanted. That did involve seeing clients when and where they wanted and that meant driving over 30,000 miles a year.

Back then, I had suddenly started to realise that the same opportunities in the UK would apply in other developing nations and within 5 years I would be a regular traveller to the Far East. Another 5 years after that, my wife, I and two daughters would emigrate to live in Singapore.

I must have known in the back of my mind that the UK would reach a point in growth that could not be sustained. The opportunities in the UK were great if you moved with the times. To prepare for that, I started to learn about Far Eastern culture, particularly that of China. Indeed I was so wrapped up in that, that I started to learn Chinese. Nowadays I can speak Chinese Mandarin very well and also read and write the language. Useful in China but totally not useful at this time in the UK. In fact my wife would describe me as like a lighthouse on top of the Pennines;brilliant but totally useless!

Now contrary to popular belief Chinese, isn't a difficult language to learn once you understand the main principles and rules. Just like anything else you may choose to learn. To begin with, I had to allocate the time, that was the main challenge.

As I was working 15 hour days it didn't leave much, however I worked out that I was spending a good 4 hours a day sat in my car travelling the length and breadth of the country. To put that time to good use I purchased a Linguaphone Chinese Mandarin language course. These were a series of books to learn the written language but most importantly for me a set of 8 two sided cassette tapes which I could play in my car and learn parrot- fashion. I would study the written language on a Saturday morning and voila the two together would be a success. Wrong! Here I am now some 32 years later still studying but I am still not completely fluent. I have had a lot of fun along the journey though and for someone who was brought up in the countryside in the UK, I suppose I have a skill ahead of many.

That skill, which was still being developed back then, was put to the test in 1993. I was asked to go and advise a very wealthy family in Taiwan, Republic of China. Without getting too political, the Republic of China is really the rightful China. The People's Republic of China is not! I won't get into a history debate here or a political one either but it is all well documented elsewhere.

Anyway, back to this wealthy family. They paid for my flight from London to Taipei. But in those days, because the UK chose not to formally recognise Taiwan in case they upset The People's Republic, you could not fly direct. So that meant a flight with British Airways to Amsterdam and then China Airlines (that was Taiwan's Government owned national carrier) to Taipei via Bangkok, a total travel time of 23 hours.

To travel to and enter Taiwan (Republic of China) at that time you needed a visa in your passport. Unfortunately, they could not have an embassy for the political reason just mentioned above. So you had to drive all the way down to London with your passport and find the Free China Representative Office. It was all a bit James Bondish.

The front of the building was unassuming and on entry there were very few people about. I was directed to a window resembling the old off licence windows in public houses. The window slid open and I was asked for my passport and a letter from my sponsor in Taiwan. No forms to fill in nothing else to do except. I had to pay £20 in cash and was told that my passport with the visa would be posted back to me. The window then slammed shut and I made my way back home wondering if I would ever see my passport again.

Amazingly, my Blue passport (as they were then), complete with a neatly stamped visa upon page 5, arrived at my home address. In the coming years, I would fill this passport with visas and entry and exit stamps of some 80 territories and countries. Sadly, on renewal it would be changed to a boring burgundy red colour with the EU stamp on the front. Yuck!

The day arrived and in early March 1993, I kissed my wife and two little daughters goodbye for the first of what was to become many travels. It never became any easier to say bye, never! I hated leaving them but I had to earn money to support the lifestyle that we all wanted.

It was a dreadfully long flight. The service on board the first leg to Amsterdam was awful with British Airways but it all perked up once on the China Airlines flight. Food and drink a plenty accompanied with in-flight movies. I even got upgraded to first class. Unfortunately, this wasn't so good because on board were the whole Sheffield United Football Team all going for a jolly to Bangkok for the weekend. Still at least once they disembarked, the last leg to Taiwan would be peaceful and indeed it was as in Bangkok the whole of the cabin where I was filled up with Thai monks dressed in their saffron robes. They were going on a jolly to Taipei, well some sort of pilgrimage anyway. I slept the rest of the journey.

On arrival in Taipei I was mesmerised. The airport was massive and all the signs were in Chinese. I could understand some of them, well exit, entry and toilets. In fact, the later was the first place I was to visit in Taiwan, a public airport toilet. Bliss.

Going through customs was easy and seamless as was reclaiming my bag from the carousel. One of the reasons it was so quiet is that back then air travel in this part of the world was for the very wealthy, and of course, for monks. The airport had been recently renovated with the expectation of higher visitor numbers in the future.

As I made my way to the car hire desk, I noticed a lot of signage for 'Air Raid Sheltar'. Yes spelt in English just like that, incorrectly. Why? Not the spelling, I was soon to learn that the Taiwanese just wrote English like it sounded and were influenced by the American way of spelling English. But why an air raid shelter?

I later learned that Taiwan was on alert and had been since 1948 in case The People's Republic (they called them the Mainland) were to attack. Not on this visit, I hoped, as the UK had no diplomatic connections (any formal ones anyway since 1972) at that time and I would be stuck.

The mobile phone I had bought with me worked. I knew it would, as Taiwan was one of the places you could use a mobile telephone using international roaming. I took the opportunity to call my wife to tell her I was safe and well. She was happy to hear I was but not happy to receive my call as I had forgotten the UK was 8 hours behind and so it was only 3am there! That was one of two reasons I wished I hadn't used it.

The other reason is that back then you paid for your calls by the minute and using it in Taiwan, as indeed any other countries where you could, meant you were 'roaming'. We probably all know today that means using your mobile telephone in another country or territory outside of your own. Back then, the calls within Taiwan on that device were 70p a minute to a Taiwan number but £3.20 per minute back to the UK. So this leads me to the second reason I wished I had not used the phone during that trip; when I got home the next mobile telephone bill I received was for £486.22. OUCH! I still have it framed above my desk.

Right, back to Taipei airport. Using my new found skill in Chinese, I found the car hire desk and also the nice lady from Hertz dressed in a smart yellow and grey uniform. She was surprised to see me. Firstly, because they did not get many Western people hiring cars and secondly because I could speak Chinese Mandarin. I must have done OK because I understood almost everything she said and collected the set of documents and maps she handed to me. She escorted me outside into the car park where my white Ford something was stood. Wow it was hot, I thought, with the weather at about 25C. Much hotter than the 5C in London where I had commenced my journey. Also, the stale pollution of car exhausts in the air, this all met me full in the face when the sliding glass doors opened from the lovely air conditioned airport into what was going to be my home for the next 10 days. This was an experience I would experience many times in the future when travelling, particularly in most Asian cities.

The 'Hertz' lady opened the door of the white Ford (on the wrong side as Taiwan drive as do Europe and the USA on the wrong side of the road) and proceeded to tell me about driving within Taiwan. I politely interrupted and explained I was an experienced driver of many years and I knew what all the controls did. I just wanted to be on my way. Bad mistake!

She handed me the keys to the vehicle and I thanked her and bid her a farewell. Right, I started the vehicle and switched on the lovely cool air conditioning. I sat for a moment to get my bearings and then realised the first of many different driving conditions I would soon have to deal with... the fuel gauge was nearly empty. Apparently back then that is how you handed the car back as the last renter of the vehicle had obviously done. That would mean I needed to find a petrol station as soon as possible.

Secondly and indeed not surprisingly the map she had given to me was all in Chinese. As I glanced up, I also noticed the road signage was written in Chinese too. Well at least I have learned written Chinese thank goodness and the signs were mainly of international pictorial standards.

I then decided to telephone my clients and tell them I had arrived. They had arranged the hire car at my request as I advised in advance that I didn't like taking public transport and also I did not want to put them to any trouble by them meeting me inside the airport. I wished then, as I have a number of times since, that I wasn't such a stubborn independent sod! At the end of a long flight, you do not want to be navigating your way around a strange land with unfamiliar sign posts, climate change and the apprehensive feeling that you may never arrive.

The phone rang out giving the American style ringtone. It was answered by a lady who could speak very good English. It turned out she was the client's Phillipine maid (actually they were called a domestic helper or amah and most professional/wealthy people had one). She explained that neither Sir nor Madam were at home but that they were expecting me. She did not drive so she could not help me with directions.

Right, all that done, I decided to take off my English overcoat. My God, that was why I was so hot. Typical Englishman abroad, I still had my jacket and tie on which I always did and still do today when travelling. The tie these days though, is usually not worn but kept handily ready in my right hand jacket pocket together with the Rennies and diarrhea capsules. Fortunately for the reader, my medical needs are a story for another time.

I put the vehicle into D as it was an automatic and moved forward towards the end of the car park. The barrier of the carpark lifted like some portcullis in the safety of a castle and revealed the highway ahead. Would this be like a lamb to the slaughter?

Ahead, I could see the sign, (in Chinese of course) for PETROL well actually it said 'China Petrol' but written in Chinese. Back then, in Taiwan, everything was China this or Taiwan as all products were controlled by the Taiwanese Government. There was no choice in brands or competition. Even the flight I had arrived on had no competition; it was The Government Airline, China Airlines.

I drove onto the garage forecourt and got out of the vehicle and walked towards the fuel pump. At once I was almost pounced upon by a forecourt attendant dressed in a red white and blue China Petrol uniform. He told me to get back in the vehicle as garages in Taiwan were not self service and that he would attend to refulling the car. This was an introduction to Asia as my future travel revealed service standards far more friendly and superior to the West.

Whilst I sat in the car, another man dressed in uniform asked me to open the bonnet. He checked the oil and water which

I thought was crazy as I had only just collected the vehicle. I did not protest as a third person again in uniform cleaned the already clean windows on the vehicle. I decided to switch on the car radio and was surprised that it was an English radio station called ICRT (Independent Commercial Radio of Taiwan) complete with English, well American speakers.

Actually, I was to find out later this radio station was a remnant of the Vietnam war whereby American servicemen would be flown to Taiwan for R and R or be taken there to a military hospital if injured. The station was set up to broadcast to the foreign troops by the US Army. After the war had ended in 1976, some of the servicemen decided to stay in Taiwan (many of whom had met Taiwanese ladies). The song playing on the radio at that moment was 'If you leave me now' by Chicago. Again this was to be another place and time I would remember forever. Lovely song that, although my listening experiences were disturbed by a tap on the window by the attendant who had finished refueling the vehicle. The other two attendants had disappeared and the car bonnet had been closed shut. "All done" he said in Chinese "That will be 510 dollars" and he stepped aside as he pointed to the petrol pump dial which backed up his statement. "My God!" I thought "petrol is very expensive here and I don't have that amount of cash on me." I offered him my mastercard which he examined. He called over the other two attendants who also examined the card turning it over and smiling. The first attendant came back to the car and handed me the card explaining that they did not accept these cards as a method of payment.

I was to find out later that money was strictly controlled by the government at the time. They did not accept foreign credit or debit cards. In fact when it came to changing any money, including the £700 I had brought in Thomas Cooks' travellers cheques, you had to go to one of only 3 government approved banks on the island.

He asked me to move off the forecourt as my financial enquiries had now caused a long line of traffic queuing out of the forecourt and onto the road. He requested I park by the service shop and enter to discuss the matter with a member of the petrol service staff. To cut a long story short I discovered that the $510 was not of course American dollars but the currency of Taiwan which was called the New Taiwanese Dollar or NT$ for short. I worked out in my head that there were NT$143 to One British pound and therefore the $510 worth of petrol was about £3.56? Surely not? that would have cost at least £40 in the UK back then to fill an empty tank to full. But no it was true the greedy British

Government taxed (and indeed still does) tax the British motorist through the roof on petrol and diesel.

The Taiwan Government back then took an opposite approach and therefore that fact plus the excellent exchange rate (if you were British) meant a staggering 90% less for the same product. Added to this Britain had its own fuel reserves where Taiwan had to import most of its fuel.

Anway, I took a crisp £5 note from my wallet and offered it to exchange for the petrol in the car. The attendant made a series of phone calls and asked me to sit down . I did so and was immediately offered a cup of tea. That was most welcome as I hadn't had a drink since leaving the aircraft three hours ago now. It was strange tasting tea and served black with no sugar or milk. That is another thing I would become used to on this trip and in the years ahead. In fact so much so that even today I often drink my tea without milk.

I had been in the garage now well over an hour, when yet another uniformed person appeared. She spoke excellent English and explained she was the station manager. She further explained she was married to an Englishman who she had met 5 years previously whilst studying at Birmingham university in the UK. As a side note she and her British husband were to become good friends of mine. She recognised the £5 note as being legal tender and told the staff to accept it at once. The cashier apologised profusely for the delay and went to hand me some change. I told them I had not been inconvenienced and told her to keep the change.

Before I left, and in a quiet corner of the office, I asked the lady I had just met to change £50 to NTS. She did so with pleasure, smiling as she explained she could use that when they travelled to visit her husband's relatives in the UK. At this point, I have to say that that £50 was to last me the whole of the next 10 days.

"Right, let's get on", I thought, " I must complete my journey" as I had now been travelling for well over 24 hours and did not smell too good. I took out the map and looked at the best route, memorised the 10 miles or so trip and again put the vehicle into 'D', mirror signal maneuver and off I went again.

Taiwan is a little like the USA as regards road layout. They prefer a grid system to city planning and so it is easier to follow a route than in Europe whereby they have more twists and bends in the roads. The disadvantage was that they do not like roundabouts, as with the USA, there are traffic lights a plenty. Every half a mile or so you grind to a halt as yet another red light at another interchange impedes your progress. So that 10 miles took me a further 2 hours. This was mainly due to the stop, start and traffic jams of Biblical proportions. However the traffic menace I encountered most were motorbikes.

In England, I have always been a keen motorcyclist although these days just for pleasure on a Sunday morning. However in Taipei at that time (as with most Asian cities) motorcycles of every description were everywhere and outnumbered cars and other vehicles by what seemed like 500 to 1. They would come from nowhere like wasps buzzing around my vehicle, cutting in front and performing lots of other cunning stunts I was not familiar with.

When you reached yet another road interchange controlled by yet another set of traffic lights they would fill all of the space to either side of you and were 10 deep in a row in front of you. The noise was deafening when the lights changed to green and all of the motorcycles seemed to move forward as fast as possible all at once. The smell of two stroke oil mixed with petrol filled the air and the car with toxic $CO_2$ fumes. Again this was something I would get used to on my Asian travels in the years ahead.

Asia had seen a massive rise in growth and wealth and had experienced in 10 years what had taken most Western countries a 100 years to achieve. Indeed, during my visits in the coming years ahead, I would be staggered to see new towns and high rise buildings erected where on my previous visit there was countryside. In a few years time all of those motorcycles would become cars as people ditched them for a safer and more luxurious way of travel.

The following year I would be working in The other China. The Peoples Republic of, crossing the border from Hong Kong by road. Similar experiences would be met except there you were not allowed to drive as foreign driving licences were not recognised. If you hired a car back then, it came complete with a driver! They also had not yet evolved to motorcycle status as push bikes were the norm and I am not kidding when I say there were millions of them everywhere. Within 5 years, the landscape there would begin to look like Taiwan but on a massive scale with new super six lane highways and clever urban planning. In my time, I saw the bicycles evolve to motorcycles and then motor cars. It had all been well planned and designed with the future in mind.

When I looked at what they carried on the motorcycles I was astounded. Boxes piled as much as 10 high, bricks, dead animals being taken to be butchered, whole families of up to six people on the same machine. I mean really, a rider on the seat with the smallest child on the handlebars, two sat on the petrol tank and the mother riding pillion sometimes with two children in her arms. As I drove, I really had to be careful not to collide with any of them.

I was, by now, absolutely shattered and probably suffering with the effects of the worst air pollution my poor tired body had experienced to date. Thankfully, I arrived at my final destination of Number 9, Alley 6, Roosevelt Road, Taipei, Taiwan, Republic of China. I drove the car through some wrought iron gates that must have been opened ready for my arrival. This would be my home and place of employment for the next 9 nights.

I was greeted, as I stepped out of the car, by the Phillipine maid I had spoken to earlier on the telephone. She helped me with my baggage from the car and showed me into the house and (more importantly) showed me to the room I would be staying in.

At last I could remove my stinky clothes and have a shower. After that, all I would want is to sleep. But that was not to be. As I was untying my shoe laces and trying to prize off my shoes from my swollen feet, there was a knock on the bedroom door which then flew open to reveal my hosts.

They were a wealthy Taiwaniese couple, married for the last 32 years they said, although the wife only looked about that age and he must have been in his sixties. He was a senior member of the ruling political party the KMT (Kuomintang). Again, readers here will need to look that up on Google as I do not wish to get political or mention any names at this point.

Needless to say, they had arranged a welcome diner at one of the nicest hotels I had ever been to at that time. The Lai Lai Sheraton in Taipei. This was booked for 30 minutes hence and would involve me being the guest of honour in a privately booked dining suite together with 35 other guests.

In Chinese culture back then, people tended to judge you on your appearance (I am sure they still do) and observe your business etiquette. I had read about this beforehand and indeed to comply, I made sure I still looked fine even after my travels thus far. I checked my business cards. Never run out! Plus they were all in pristine condition and printed on both sides. One in English and one in Chinese. I placed about 50 of them into an expensive looking, silver coloured business card holder upside down. The reason for that is when I was introduced to someone I could offer them my business card the correct way. However, remembering not to do that until they had handed them theirs first and I had pretended to read what was upon it. Unfortunately by now I could hardly focus my weary bloodshot eyes.

I put my tie back on and my navy blue suit jacket, then I emptied half the contents of a bottle of Polo aftershave, which I splashed over my clothes to disguise the body odours (one I had purchased about 30 hours ago in an Amsterdam Airport duty free shop). Then I was shown down to a waiting black Cadillac Limousine and my hosts sat in the back with me as we moved through the evening Taipei traffic jams to the Lai Lai Sheraton Hotel.

I cannot remember much about that event other than I met and was greeted by so many people it all became a blur. I hoped I had made a good impression as I was treated like royalty and felt I was representing my country.

I never got to remove my shoes until another 3 hours later when I would sink into my bed having had a really long hot shower. The former would happen but not the later as when we arrived back at the house there had been a power cut. This meant there was no hot water or in fact any water as that was pumped into the property by an electric pump.

Despair was setting in especially as I had cleverly bid my hosts a goodnight in, what I thought, was good Chinese Mandarin. But a few days later I was corrected on my pronunciation on Wan Aan (goodnight) as my pronunciation had actually meant 'I kiss you both'. Well I didn't do that but that first night earned me a lot of chuckles from this lovely family and most of the hosts earlier that evening.

During that first night I think, I must have slept deeply for about 4 hours. I awoke about 2.30am as I needed the loo.. "Still no lights," I thought as I reached out for the switch by my bedside, which failed to switch on anything. So I fumbled my way to the bathroom. Fortunately I had noted the bathroom's exact location earlier in the afternoon in the light, when I could see it. This meant I could navigate there in the low light and complete my business in a most efficient and speedy manner.

I could hear thunder from outside and soon the whole house was lit up by intermittent bright flashes of lightning. It felt hot and sticky as the air conditioning was not working due to the power cut. As I slowly felt my way back to my room, I could hear the rain now lashing against the windows. All of a sudden had a great idea, in fact maybe a flash of inspiration brought on by the lightning. This had not ceased and left me wide awake now.

I could not hear anything or anyone moving within the house. Therefore, I understood all of the household to be asleep. I still stank of body odour as it would soon be 48 hours since I last had a shower. So, armed with a bar of soap and my towel, I wandered down stairs and gingerly opened the front door so as not to wake anyone.

Outside, was a huge tiled courtyard and I could just see my trusty hire car at the far side in the faded light. Without further ado, I took off my shorts and vest and stood on the courtyard completely naked in the heavy rain. I was amazed at how warm the rain was and stood there washing myself down with the bar of soap. "God! That felt so good," I thought as I washed off all the ravages of the last 48 hours. I had never used soap to wash my hair before but even that felt great.

Just as I was washing the last bits of naked flesh, there was a big flash and a metallic high pitched sound. I realised the electricity had just come back on. I could hear the whir of all the air conditioning units bursting back into life. Fortunately, there were no bright lights to light up my night time activity, thank goodness.

I made my way back under the porch where I had put my towel on the back of a chair that had been left out on the porch, dried myself off and made my way back into the house, closing the door behind me with my towel wrapped tightly around me to avoid any embarrassment if any other night owls had descended the stairs.

I could neither hear nor see anyone as I made my way sneakily back to my room. I felt clean and could smell my freshness as I put on a fresh pair of shorts and a clean T shirt. Back under the covers I sank as the room was starting to feel cold with the lovely air conditioned breeze filling the room and driving out the sticky heat.

It was to be 1pm when I next woke up. 1pm? I don't think I have ever woken up so late in all my life. Thinking about it though, it would only be 5am in the UK so about right. After all my travels and experiences thus far, I must have been tired. I started to dress, when I heard a soft knock on the door. It was the maid. "Mr David" she called. "I hope you are fine? I have placed a cup of tea by your door when you are ready"

I replied in Chinese "xie xie ni" to which she said "you are welcome but I can't speak Chinese!" However she had understood my thanks. She then said " Sir and Madam will be waiting to eat lunch with you downstairs in half an hour.

I have placed towels and shower gel in the bathroom when you are ready." I replied "Many thanks, I will see you later". With that I could hear her move away from the door and I opened the door, reaching down for the most welcome breakfast tea, well afternoon tea by now.

I showered quickly as I was already cleanish from the night before. I knew today was a rest day so when I got back to my bedroom I put on smart, but casual clothes. Making my way downstairs I saw Mr and Mrs Lee sitting at the large dining table. There were two girls with them and the maid.

As I bid them a good afternoon they looked at me giggling. Odd I thought. Mr and Mrs Lee introduced the girls as Mai-Ling and Mai-Song and explained that they were Mr Lee's daughters. They were very neatly dressed in matching colours and aged about 15 or 16. When I spoke to them, they again giggled covering their mouths with their right hands. Mr Lee told them to say hello to me and they duly obliged. He then clapped his hands and they were gone! Like two butterflies flying away to some other part of this house.

Mr Lee beckoned for me to sit down whereupon a most huge lunch was served into the middle of the table. The Lees watched me using chopsticks and were, I hope, impressed.

After lunch, the Lees continued to sit with me at the table and handed me a piece of paper onto which they had typed an agenda for the days ahead. The main reason for this visit was to advise them upon investments and tax planning. Back then, it was challenging for Taiwanese natives to be able to move money outside of the country, which is where my international expertise was to be used. Mr Lee had four brothers who also needed my advice and they had been factored into that agenda. The Lees also wanted me to spend time with their teenage daughters and teach them, where time allowed, English. The rest of my stay would involve me being presented at various functions to in effect show me off as this strange curio of a ginger haired Englishman.

After our discussions, Mr Lee said he needed a quiet word with me. He ushered me into a room off the dining room which was kitted out as his office. Some office it was too, with oak panels and tartan wall coverings. It looked like the interior of a Scottish castle, complete with an open fireplace (although you would never need this on a sub-tropical island, surely) and beautiful oak desks. All imported from Scotland he told me.

On one of the desks, was a computer. The older type with a large tower unit complete with keyboard and a very large white plastic VDU. He asked me to sit as he wanted me to see something. He pressed a button on the keyboard and a video, in black and white started to play on the screen.

I noticed the character shown in the video at once. It was a naked man on a patio standing outside in a shower of rain. I mean there was nothing left to the imagination. I suddenly felt myself filled with bright red embarrassment and realised what the girls had been giggling at earlier...it was ME!

Unfortunately for me, the patio in question was fitted with a high tech (for that time) security camera and as the electricity had come back on during my night time excursion, had illuminated me in fine Infrared glory. Fortunately though, he took the whole episode in good spirits as he laughed loudly requesting next time if I could use the bathroom provided. He also went on to explain his wife and the maid had found it all so amusing too and that he couldn't wait to show family and friends.

This again was one of those moments in your life where you remember the time, day and place forever in your memory. I wished for the ground to open up and swallow me. After my sincere apologies and pleading with him to delete the video, we went and drank tea together back in the dining room.

As a side note, I do think he probably still has that video footage. During the course of the next few days, I received many cautious looks and giggles as I was introduced to the Lees' various friends, relatives and business folk. On one occasion, I heard someone say in Chinese, "Is that him? I didn't recognise him with his clothes on!" The joys of understanding Chinese Mandarin.

That first business trip was the first of many and like many things you do for the first time stand out in your memory forever. I think it was to shape me forever and change the way I think about things.

In the coming years on many future trips I would be exposed to many new experiences which would include an earthquake, a four day typhoon, finding a venomous snake in my washing machine, an air flight where the aircraft turned upside down, getting trapped in a lift and being evacuated from a high rise building when I was on the 94th floor and having to use the staircase. Oh, and not to mention being shot at with live ammunition, stories for another time though. I am sure everyone has these or similar experiences. For me however they made me what I am today. Whatever that maybe.

## **Fit 5 Everything will be alright in the end. If it'snot alright, it is not yet the end...**

Towards the later part of the 1990s, I had travelled all over the globe with my work and was getting to the point where I was missing my wife and children very much. Most of my work was in the Far East. After a long discussion lasting about 5 minutes, my wife and I decided that the best way forward was to move out to the Far East to live.

The planning for that massive event for the four of us was another 4 months in the making. We decided to burn all our bridges and sell our home in the UK, so making a new family life in, of all places, Singapore. We chose there initially as it was a safe and a very cosmopolitan place to go and emigrate to. The schools followed the English system and so my two daughters, in theory, would have no problem in adapting. Also the spoken language was English. And so we waited until the school they attended broke up for the summer holiday which would give us 6 weeks in which to move, settle down and for them to start the Singaporean school at the start of the Autumn term.

This period was to be a wonderful experience for us all. My work would be exactly the same except, when I finished for the day, I would actually go home and be with my family. I already had business connections out there, so being part of the life would be an easy transition. We had already visited many places but only for 2 week holidays so this was going to be great. To watch a new world but through the eyes of my two daughters. Truly exciting and amazing.

And so it was to be, that we sold everything and left the UK on a Singaporean Airlines flight to a new home in the tropics. The place we would quickly get used to and a place that would mean so much to us in the years ahead. It was all going to be a long way from the changeable British countryside we all knew so well.

One of the problems we faced on arrival was that we only could stay 30 days as tourists. Also we had nowhere to live. That meant living in a hotel initially in one of the most expensive places in the world.

We didn't want to tie our capital up at this time so we decided to rent a property. As the Far East is very different to the UK, we decided to rent a 3 bedroom apartment with a swimming pool and complete with it's own security guards. However this was over kill as Singapore is one of the nicest, friendliest and safest places to live in the world.

Singapore was (and probably still is) like a parallel universe. You know you are abroad straight away but everything seems very familiar. Probably because of the British influence up to 9 August 1965.

All of the signage and street names are in English. The official language is English although you quickly got used to Singlish, a strange mix of English, Hokkien, Malay, Teochew, Cantonese and Tamil. So street names like Newton Road, Raffles Place, Ballester Road and Orchard Road are a remnant from the past. Not to mention the Singapore districts for example: Woodlands, Marine Parade and MacPherson.

We rented our first property in Bukit Timah Road near to Newton MRT (Mass Rapid Transit) Railway Station. For the next six months, this wonderful cheap to use and very safe and efficient railway system would take us everywhere we needed to be until we obtained our first motor car there.

Now driving a car in Singapore is very easy as the road rules are similar to Britain including when you drive into Malaysia across a causeway. We used to do this most weekends to enjoy a similar but different culture.

To own a car in Singapore isn't easy. You cannot just go out and purchase one like you can in most countries. I would say that Singapore is one of the most expensive countries in which to own and run your own vehicle. Firstly, you have to buy a certificate of entitlement which is eye wateringly expensive. Then the vehicle itself which is much more expensive than the UK. Finally the actual running costs as petrol is more expensive than in the UK. Also almost everywhere you go there is a structure of road pricing similar to the congestion charge in London. In fact London copied the Singapore model. With all of that taken care of (and a depleted bank current account) it is very useful with a family and living in a hot tropical country to own one.

Anyway, back to that first house. As it was rented it came fully furnished, which was useful as we had had all of our possessions put into storage in the UK for the time being. We were shown a number of very nice apartments before we chose the one near Newton MRT.

Two strange things within each property that we weren't used to at the time, were firstly The Armoury! Well that's what it sounded like from the female estate agent who showed us around. So we thought it was a room within the place where you kept guns and ammunition. But wait, Singapore did not have guns like they do in America, so what did she mean? Well, it was simple. Most people had a maid (called an ahmah) or domestic helper. I mentioned this earlier in my memoirs when travelling to Taiwan some years before. So what the lady estate agent meant (actually she was one of a few people that became good friends who could not speak English) was an ahmahrey which is a room where your maid (ahmah) would stay and live.

However it was to be another 6 months before we decided to employ domestic help as we simply weren't used to having another person clean up after us and cook meals. You do soon change to that way of thinking though in the heat out there.

The second item that made us smile was the introduction to Lady Susan. The estate agent made several references to this each time gesturing to the dining room. However it wasn't until we entered that room that the penny dropped. The culture there is, as in many Asian countries, to share the food around a circular table. In the centre of the table is a device that you place the food upon and it can be turned around to face the dish to which you want to select and move with chopsticks to your plate or bowl. This was called a Lazy Susan not a Lady Susan. I must say, in my life until then, I had never heard this word. I had of course dined many times in Asia using that device.

Life in Singapore was lovely. After 6 months and a lot of form filling we obtained our citizenship and permanent residency status. The hours I worked were long but I was always back home each night. Singapore also has a lot of public holidays as it is truly a multicultural society. That meant the Government respects all creeds and religions and the special religious holidays. However in the beginning there were many days I took the children to school or went to my office and found it all locked up because of yet another public holiday. Still the swimming pool had a lot of use.

The time in Singapore was exquisite watching the children grow and the strange world into which I had brought them compared to life in the UK. Time never stops does it? Indeed it seemed to move faster there without the four seasons to gauge the passage of time by. It was either hot, very hot or excruciating hot and that heat accompanied by the most vicious and loud afternoon thunderstorms.

In an instant, another chapter of my life was to close as the 20th Century drew close to an end. Yes, it would soon be a new millennium and how fitting that the 31 December 1999 was spent in the ex British territory. We walked down from our abode to a viewing place near one of the two Singapore harbours. On the stroke of Midnight there was cheering and shouting as many ships out at sea let off fog horns and their red emergency distress flares.It was an amazing sight and sound and made me reflect on my life thus far and the cautious exciting optimism of what was to lie ahead.

As I write, almost at the end of my memories thus far, I still have not fulfilled ALL of my life's ambitions. Most, yes but one big one still remains. If you have not guessed yet, it is to travel into space. Whilst it is not inconceivable that with what remains of my life I may still do this, I think it would rather be as a space tourist and not as a professional astronaut. Also, I would not be the first British one as both a man and a woman have already beat me to that claim. Oh well, as a wise person once said about life, if you plan and aim for the moon, should you miss then you will be amongst the stars. I would like to think that I am one of those stars but that is not for me to judge.

THE END, WELL NOT QUITE...........

## Epilogue - This Grandad's brief history

David has been married to the same woman since 1980 and she continues to put up with him. They have 2 children and 3 Grandchildren.

Following a professional training in business studies at college and then his first paid full time job in a steel works, David joined the Inland Revenue in 1981 as a Tax Officer Higher Grade. This position meant he was responsible for the computation of tax for directors and higher paid individuals. From here he joined the Anglia Building Society as a Branch Manager.

In December 1985, he left Anglia and commenced working for the Bank of China in Birmingham as an Independent Financial Adviser/Private Banker. His advice covered: Financial Planning for Limited Companies and their directors and, on the domestic side, he advised on a very wide range of financial services including pensions, life assurance, mortgages, offshore trusts, stocks and shares, unit trusts and taxation matters.

In 1992, he became responsible for managing two of the company's branches in Taiwan and Hong Kong and marketing financial services to expats and foreign nationals. Soon after he was appointed Director, South East Asia based in Singapore.

Sadly in January 2005 his wife became very ill and they were forced to return to the UK. The organization gave him a retirement package and so he reluctantly returned to the UK.

Since then, David made a career in the UK working with local businesses that wanted to trade in and with the Far East. However, he always wanted to write a book and become an astronaut. One of those goals still remains....

Printed in Great Britain
by Amazon